The Cameliers

The Cameliers
A Classic Account of the Australians
of the Imperial Camel Corps During
the First World War in the Middle East

Oliver Hogue
(Trooper Bluegum)

The Cameliers: A Classic Account of the Australians of the Imperial Camel Corps During the First World War in the Middle East
by Oliver Hogue

Published by Leonaur Ltd

Text in this form copyright © 2008 Leonaur Ltd

ISBN: 978-1-84677-524-6 (hardcover)
ISBN: 978-1-84677-523-9 (softcover)

http://www.leonaur.com

Publisher's Notes

The opinions expressed in this book are those of the author and are not necessarily those of the publisher.

Contents

Acknowledgements	9
Foreword	13
The Soldier	15
The Sister	21
The Soldier	27
The Sister	32
Romani—1	38
Romani—2	43
The Soldier	47
The Soldier	52
The Sister	57
The Soldier	63
The Ball—1	68
The Ball—2	74
The Sister	80
The Soldier	85
The Soldier	90
The Sister	96
The Soldier	102
The Sister	108
Allenby—1	115
Allenby—2	120

Allenby—3	123
Allenby—4	126
Allenby—5	130
The Soldier	134
Camel Races	140
The Soldier	148
The Soldier	152
Kantara	157
The Soldier	161
Sister and Soldier	168
L'Envoi	174

To
The Honourable James Alexander Hogue
An Australian Patriot

This little record of the deeds —and misdeeds—of the Imperial Camel Corps in Egypt, Sinai, and Palestine is dedicated with sincere filial affection by

The Author

Acknowledgements

Some of the verses and a few of the incidents in this volume have appeared in *The Sydney Morning Herald, The Bulletin, The Kia Ora Cooee, London Opinion, Barrak,* etc. The greater part of the story is now published for the first time.

O. H.

To My Camel

You're an ugly smellful creature:
You're a blot upon the plain:
I have seen Mohamed beat you,
And it gave me little pain.
You're spiteful and you're lazy,
You'd send a white man crazy,
But I reckon you're a daisy
When the Turks come out again.

Your head is most unsightly,
And so is your humpy back;
I hear you roaring nightly,
When you're loading for the track.
You're bow-legged and you're bandy,
But in this desert sandy
It's as well to have you handy:
You're a mighty useful hack.

You shake me something cruel
When you try to do a trot;
I've got to take my gruel,
But you make it very hot:
I've somehow got a notion
That your Humpty-Dumpty motion
Is worse than on the ocean,
It's a nasty way you've got.

It's a sun-scorched land, the East is,
So we need you when we trek:
My old prad a better beast is,
But he'd soon become a wreck:
You thirst a week unblinking,
And when I see you drinking,
You always set me thinking:
Lord, I wish I had your neck.

Foreword

This book will be placed before the public in the midst of world-wide jubilance consequent upon the termination of the bloodiest and most unjustifiable war in the history of mankind. Soon we trust the ban of the censor will be lifted and we shall be permitted to know more of those things which a curious public has been hungering for during the last four years. I do not refer to matters of ordinary gossip, but the revealing of all those circumstances leading up to great decisions, the explanations of misfortunes and the endless tales of individual heroism. Unfortunately, such subjects are shorn of much of their interest through delay in publication. The *Cameliers* is, therefore, issued at an opportune moment, following closely upon the triumphant progress of General Allenby's army in Palestine, with the sound of his victory still ringing in our ears, when we are better enabled to appreciate details. The *Cameliers* presents a stirring picture of the arduous conditions of campaigning in that historical country in Egypt and the Sinai desert, of the inequality of numbers and equipment in the early days, of the gradual organisation of a magnificent mobile force, of hardship nobly endured, of courage and heroism daily manifested, and the final securing of the power to move forward culminating in the great sweep northwards which immediately preceded the surrender of Turkey.

The book is full of interest. It is well written, and appeals to the sympathy of all readers. Mr. Oliver Hogue is an Australian by birth and training. He is the son of Hon. James Hogue, one of the pioneers of Australian journalism, and who for many years was a well-known figure in the public life of his State. The son followed in the literary footsteps of his father, and has already contributed freely with his pen under the name of "Trooper Bluegum." Shortly after the outbreak of war he volunteered for service with the Australian Forces, and has undergone some years of continuous and arduous soldiering in Egypt and the East—an experience which fits him for a truthful reproduction of the life of a soldier in these sandy wastes.

I venture to commend this work of Trooper Bluegum not only to the general public as the attractive representation of aspects of one of the successful "side shows" of the Allies, but more especially to Australian readers as a record of the doings of the Light Horse Regiments and other Australian Units, who to their regret were unable to share in the horrors and glory of the Western Front, but have nevertheless proved themselves able in Palestine to maintain the high reputation won by the Australians as fighters in this great war.

C. S. Wade
Sidney House
11th November 1918.

Chapter 1

The Soldier

We hated the thought of 'em. We hated the sight of 'em. We hated the smell of 'em. We hated the shape of 'em. The very idea of association with such brutes was hateful to us—at first.

But the time was not far distant when we were to forget all our initial antipathies. Familiarity bred content. The law of compensation was in operation. A beast with so many obvious vices as a camel must have some compensating virtues. But it *did* take time to unearth them.

Those of us who were Light Horsemen loved our horses. It was a big wrench to go to Gallipoli without them. It was still harder to part with them finally when we joined the Imperial Camel Corps. For no Australian really loves a camel. It isn't done. All one can hope to do is to appreciate his good points and envy his thirst.

The good points manifested themselves sparingly, one at a time. The camel was strong. He was tractable—if properly handled. He could go thirsty for a week or more uncomplainingly. He could carry food for himself and his rider for many days in the wilderness. He was easily caught, and hobbled, and tethered. He gave little or no trouble at night. He would eat out of your hand—sometimes. Sometimes he tried to eat your hand.

Long before we saw our new mounts we knew all about them—or thought we did. The cognoscenti saw to that. In every camp somehow there seems to be a little coterie of 'know alls', old soldiers to whom nothing is hidden in the heavens above or the earth beneath or the waters under the earth. In course of time we estimated these gentlemen at their true value, and found for the most part they had been kicked out of their units for worthlessness, or had deliberately chosen the soft and safe job at the details. But at first we listened open-mouthed to their terrible tales of thrilling adventures and miraculous escapes: the buckjumpers they had cowed, the ferocious Bedouins they had captured single-handed. Gladly we new chums bought them beer at the canteen, and refilled their pint pots again and again that their tongues might be loosened and the worst be told. And at night, after 'Lights out', as the wild wind off the Mokattam Hills wafted us the aroma of camel, we lay awake and thought apprehensively of the morrow. Towards morning we dreamed nasty dreams in which wild camels chased us, yet never caught us, though our feet seemed glued to the ground.

The boys of the I.C.C. looked back with a tolerant smile at those early days at Abbassia; the early morning parades, the mountains of equipment that were heaped upon us, the wild and woolly shivoos in Cairo in the evenings, the joy-rides round Heliopolis and Mattarieh, the realistic sham-fights on the Virgins' Breasts, the preliminary treks out to the desert in full marching order, with stragglers dotting the sand as far as the eye could reach, the strafes we got and never earned, the many more strafes we richly deserved but somehow escaped. We thought we were rather slow making the acquaintance of our camels, till one day a senior officer rode up and watched our company at mounted drill. We didn't know if he were a general or what, but we all bucked up a bit and performed the various evolutions with precision of Life Guards—almost. When we dismounted for 'smoko" the officer aforesaid cantered up and inquired, "How long have you chaps had camels?"

"Two weeks exactly," he was told.

Whereat he whistled, and confided to our O.C. that he had seen a company of Cameliers who, after two months' work, were not to be compared with us.

And in all humility be it said these adaptable young Australians took to camels like ducks to water. Admittedly their language, when a camel went mangoon, was simply shocking, and, I fear me, a few of them did drink a little more beer than was absolutely necessary. The captious critics will tell you this, and will dwell on the fact that a few thousand wild Australians on a couple of occasions tried to mop up Cairo and paint Alexandria crimson. Yet if you put these boyish follies in the scale, and against them set off their whole-souled patriotism, their imperturbable good-humour, their hardihood, their sturdy democracy, their supreme contempt of death and danger, then you see the Anzac in true perspective. His idiosyncrasies are forgotten, and he stands forth a virile and unique figure on the battle-fields of Sinai.

It was not all plain sailing with those camels. Several men badly bitten went to hospital. A few were thrown hard on the gravel-strewn plain. Others were kicked, and the padded foot of the camel is much harder than it looks. One unlucky officer achieved fame—or notoriety—by being knocked off his camel by an aeroplane. There was plenty of excitement when a mangoon beast broke loose and cleared the parade-ground. The Cameliers cheered and roared when a hapless Gyppie fled before the onslaught of a mad camel. But they forgot to cheer when Stinker swung round and charged in their direction. It was *sauve qui peut* and devil take the hindmost. Then half a dozen men with a long rope, or one hero with an iron bar, was the only thing to stop the camel.

There was one man-killer there with a most unsavoury reputation. He had killed a few men and sent several to hospital. Anon he went on trek with an Anzac battalion, and after a spell of decent behaviour broke out again and threatened to slaughter a whole section.

He was laid out temporarily with a crack on the skull, but the rider was taking no more chances. Next day he loitered behind on the trek, blew the camel's brains out, and reported to the O.C. that the camel had died of a broken heart.

We were, while at Abbassia, lectured on camels. We studied their habits and habitat. We learned how, centuries ago, the Persian Camelry had routed the Lydian Cavalry, and how the Roman horses fled before the North African Cameliers. We inquired into the feeding of camels, and the reason for their prolonged abstinence and their wonderful thirst. Now and then we ate camels, though the obliging mess caterers assured us it was veal.

We were quite as careless as the average soldier, and no more moral. So we were always losing saddles, or fantasses, or dhurra bags, or brushes, or head-ropes. And we had to make good the deficiencies.

But we never thieved—at least not within our own company lines.

True, it was no great crime to commandeer a saddle or a camel from headquarters. The commandment simply ran: "Thou shalt not be caught." And it was an easy thing for an Australian to fake a brand and disguise a camel; we managed to get a few rather decent mounts from the H.Q. lines.

Grooming and ticking did get on our nerves. There were big ticks, little ticks, and middle-sized ticks. Camels newly arrived from the desert were swarming with ticks, and we had to slaughter them—the ticks I mean; and because the job offended our sense of the aesthetic we adopted the motto for the company: "*Infra dig camelorum, ora pro nobis*"; which being translated means, perhaps, "O Lord, fancy coming to this."

Realising that all work and no play made the Anzac a dull boy, we indulged in the delightful pastime of buckshee riding. 'Buckshee' is the Australian's adaptation of 'baksheesh.' For a while the scheme worked admirably. Ostensibly for the purpose of 'trying out' our camels, we got permission from the CO. to take our camels off the lines on Sunday afternoons for short rides along the wadis. Then we grew bolder. We invited the nurses from the adjacent hospitals to ride to Mattarieh or the Gardens or Napoleon's Tower. And dozens of the boys held camel races on the desert. It was fine fun. All went swimmingly.

For six days of the week we laboured and did all our work, but on the seventh, perched on the top of our *hooshtas,* we were monarchs of all we surveyed. The only disadvantage was the proximity of telegraph wires, and the frequency with which we got caught under the chin and almost hanged for being so high up in the world.

Unhappily, *buckshee* riding came to an find all too soon. I quote from *Barrak,* the official organ of the I.C.C.

> Rumours of impending strife reached us one morning at breakfast. A senior officer proceeding 'in the execution of his duty' from Cairo to Heliopolis, the previous afternoon, had seen every lamp-post outside every pub and café, from Abbassia onwards, garlanded and festooned with camels, while a seething crowd fought and jostled round six ships of the desert riding easily at their anchors outside Heliopolis House. Disciplinary action was taken, as the saying is, and buckshee camel riding came to an end.

Anon came the exodus. Good-bye to the flesh-pots of Egypt, the bints at the Barage, the carousals at the Kursaal, the fun on the feluccas, the games at Ghezira, the nights on the Nile—and the sweet smiles of the Sisters.

A dozen times the rumour had run that we marched on the morrow. But rumour always was a lying jade. At last, however, it was dinkum. We were fully equipped—officially—and up to strength. In full marching order we formed up, and the camera fiends got very, very busy.

The general completed his inspection. A couple of magnificent camels from headquarters were unaccountably found in our lines, and these were reclaimed and culls given us in exchange. In a long column of humps we moved out into the desert.

At Abbassia all was peaceful again. The dust of our departure settled quietly on the empty huts, and Adjutant Barber breathed a sigh of intense relief as he turned to the G.O.C. and exclaimed, "Thank God they've gone."

Chapter 2

The Sister

"Sister!" cried the big, sunburnt bush-man in the third bed.

The nurse rose from the little table in the centre of the ward and noiselessly glided across to the patient.

"Well, what's wrong now, Pat?"

"Sister, will you marry me?"

"Not today, Pat, thank you. I'm frightfully busy," answered Sister, with a smile.

"If you die an old maid, you've only got yourself to blame," quoted the soldier.

"Oh well, I'll risk it."

"Then if you won't marry me, will you please have a look at this confounded ankle. Sure the bandage is too tight, or else my foot is swelling wisibly, as Sam Weller would say."

With a few deft movements she removed the offending bandage, exposing an ugly wound caused by a mauser bullet. Then in a minute or two Sister had bound up the ankle again, and the bushman did not know whether he should marvel most at her dexterity or the gentleness of her touch. "Oh, Sister darlint, I wisht I had a bullet in my other leg just for the sheer joy of watching' ye."

The nurse tried hard not to smile as she straightened the bedclothes. "Anything else now?"

"Only my heart," said the patient resignedly.

She ignored this, for every one of her eleven patients

seemed to be suffering from the same affection. Glancing round the ward as she turned her back towards the table, she caught sight of a signal of distress from the far corner.

"Well, Billjim, what's the matter with you this morning?"

Of course his name was not Billjim. That is the curious composite cognomen that has been used indiscriminately of late, and serves as a label for any of the Anzacs. But by general consent the other ten patients in Ward B4 had christened this wiry young colonial 'Billjim'. Perhaps it was because his physiognomy was curiously like unto the Australian youth depicted by that consummate artist Norman Lindsay. Perhaps it was on account of his devil-may-care disposition, or his extraordinarily elastic vocabulary, or his inveterate cigarette smoking, or his lack of reverence for staff officers, clergymen, medicoes, or silk hats. Whatever the reason, no one in the ward challenged his exclusive right to the honoured name of Billjim. To be sure the board next his bed, with the zigzag lines and the hieroglyphics, had at the top "Private Eagleton James, 1st Battn., A.I.F." But only the M.O. troubled about his official name.

"Say, what about that letter you promised to write to my bit of skirt, Sister?" he now demanded.

"It won't be too long, will it?" This in view of a host of other calls on Sister's time.

"Lor' lumme, I ain't written since I left Gallip," he replied in an aggrieved tone.

So, seating herself at the foot of his bed with pencil and pad in readiness, Sister turned to Billjim and invited him to begin.

"Come closer, Sister. I don't want that red-headed, freckled-faced coot in No. 8 to hear my love letters."

"Oh, he's asleep, I'm sure."

Loud snoring suddenly sounding from the adjacent bed only partly reassured Billjim, but without more ado he began:

"My dearest Liz.—Got that?—I hope this finds you well, as it leaves me at present.—Got that?"

Sister looked at his right arm in a sling, and thought of the shrapnel pellets in his shoulder, but she only smiled. The wounded swain proceeded:

"I'm in the 14th A.G.H.; that means Australian General Hospital.—Got that?—And they treat you bosker. I got a couple of lumps of shrapnel in my shoulder from Beachy Bill, but it ain't nothin' to cable home about.—Got that?—Why didn't you answer my letter from Lone Pine?—Got that?—I guess I'll be back into the scrum in a couple of weeks.—Got that?"

Sister smiled again. She knew better. But she scribbled on.

"We didn't do too bad over there considerin'.—Got that?—Every time we took a trench there was more trenches behind, and whenever we breasted a hill there was more hills ahead.—Got that?—But they wouldn't send old Ian nearly enough men, considerin' Winston Churchill had sent the Navy on ahead lo warn Abdul we was comin'."

"Here," exclaimed Sister, "you cannot go on criticising the High Command like that, you know."

"Who's criticism' 'em?"

"You are, of course."

"Well," replied Billjim doggedly, "what's generals for if they ain't to be criticised? What's the good of learnin' history?"

This was a poser for the amanuensis, so she meekly resumed her task. Billjim fired away, and in queer staccato phrases told his own plain tale of the glorious landing of the Anzacs on that never-to-be-forgotten morning of 25th April. There were incidents of splendid heroism and stoical endurance, yet he just kept on with no more excitement than he would have shown in describing a cricket-match or a wallaby drive. It never appeared to him as anything extraordinary. But when he described the wild charge at Lone Pine and Walker's Ridge, in the face of a veritable hail of lead, Sister forgot to write, and just sat there exclaiming, "Wonderful! Wonderful!"

"Oh, that ain't nothin'," deprecated the unimaginative warrior. "You ought to 'a seen Dally Messenger playing for Easts the season before last. O'course he wasn't any good at all. Oh no."

The epistle was finished at last. There was a blotch on one sheet where he had described thirty young Australians laid out in Brown's Dip for burial. He knew not that the blotch was caused by Sister's tears. Scanning the letter critically, he remarked, "You might put at the end, 'Please excuse bad writin'.'"

There was a sound of stifled mirth in No. 8 bed, but Sister ignored it, and did as she was bid.

"You can just sign it 'Jim,' now, and fill the rest of the sheet in with crosses," he added in most matter-of-fact tones.

A few minutes afterwards the medical officer entered, and Sister needs must accompany him on his rounds. Captain Evans was quite a brilliant young medico, and knew his job, but he had the fatal gift of 'swank,' which the Australians could not tolerate. Besides, he was head over ears in love with Sister, and did not seem to care who knew it. The Australian Eleven resented this, for they held that Sister Livingstone was their own exclusive property.

"Good morning, Sister," he greeted. "How is the Australian Eleven today—eh, what?" And he went the round of the ward, glancing at the charts, questioning here and there, attending to a few of the more serious cases, and, on the whole, behaving most affably. Then, as he concluded his tour of duty, he said to Sister, quite loud enough for several of the boys to hear, "I'm frightfully bucked today, Sister. Six serious cases in Ward 3 have recovered, and are well on the road to convalescence. And we had almost given them up."

Sister was about to murmur the usual congratulatory platitudes, when she heard Billjim say, in a stage whisper to No. 8, "That's 'cos the Doctor's always playing golf lately. It gives the fellows a chance."

At the entrance to the ward the Doctor turned and whispered, "What about dinner at Shepheard's tonight, Sister? The music will be excellent."

"I ought to write home to my old dad," she answered, half consenting.

"There's no Australian mail for over a week."

"Very well," agreed Sister, smiling. "Thanks awfully."

As the medical officer left the ward another case entered, or rather was carried in on a stretcher. One arm was swathed in lint. His face was drawn and haggard as if with pain. He was no light weight, and the stretcher-bearers who carried him upstairs were only too glad to give their burden over to the safe keeping of the ministering angel of B4. The newcomer eyed the Sister hungrily, as if he had not seen a lady for years. And once, when the Sister went to the other end of the ward for another pillow, Billjim heard the stranger exclaim, "God bless the Turk that shot me." But not a word did he say to Sister. His wound was dressed and bandaged anew; his old Light Horse uniform, torn and bloodstained, was taken away. With a sigh of great content he lay back in a nice clean bed, the first he had slept in for months and months. His name was entered in the hospital records, "Sergeant Robert Blaine, 7th A.L.H. Regiment, age 36," together with various details as to his religion, service, wounds, etc. And when all these preliminaries were satisfactorily accomplished, Sister stood smiling before him and asked, "Is there anything else I can do for you?"

He looked up at her sweet face with a concentrated attention that was rather embarrassing. The sun shining through the open window touched her golden hair till it seemed to the soldier that a halo had framed the most beautiful face he had ever seen. Frankly and fearlessly her deep blue eyes looked down on him awaiting an answer. But she had to repeat her question before he roused himself. "Well, anything else, Sergeant?"

He shook his head slowly, and instead of answering her

question said deliberately, "Do you know, I've been looking for you for thirty years."

"Oh, Sergeant Blaine, you must not start saying such silly things."

"Yet I dare swear it was the sanest thing I have ever said in all my life," he maintained.

And the irrepressible Billjim sat up in his bed and called out to No. 3, "Say, Pat, you're an 'also ran.'"

During the day Sister rather avoided the big man in No. 12, and in the evening went cheerily forth with the Doctor to join the gay throng in Cairo. But several times when the music was playing softly, she found her thoughts winging back to the hospital, and she heard a deep, musical voice saying, "I've been looking for you for thirty years."

Chapter 3

The Soldier

German agents had been rather busy out on the Tripoli frontier amongst the Senussi, with the result that several thousand tribesmen, armed with Turkish rifles and buoyed up with ridiculous hopes based on the alleged helplessness of Egypt, swooped down on Dakla and the Kharga Oasis. In course of time they were driven back to their base and smashed up by the Western Frontier Force.

But the German agents were quite satisfied. That little manoeuvre cost the Egyptian Government at least a million sterling. Also it brought some Scottish Yeomanry, Egyptian cavalry, half a flight of the Royal Flying Corps, some armoured motor-cars, and a company of Australian Cameliers right across Egypt from the Sinai front, and kept them there for six months all through a scorching sun.

Australians know what heat is. Bourke, Cloncurry, Oodnadatta, and Marble Bar are not so very far behind Cairo when it comes to real dinkum scorching weather. Still the hardy Cameliers, who had experienced a blazing drought in Central Australia, were quite prepared to accord the palm to the Sahara. They trekked for days and days and weeks and weeks. Time and again their meagre supply of water gave out, and with leathery tongues, blistered faces, and cracked, bleeding lips they staggered back to camp again. Several times it looked like a tragedy; once it was very, very nearly one.

A patrol following up the Senussi had gone just beyond the safety radius. Finally, water gave out. Two of the strongest men, after swallowing the last drop of water, made into Kharga, arriving almost dead with thirst. Water was hurriedly sent out to the patrol. When the rescuers got there, none of the patrol could speak. All their tongues were swollen up and their lips scorched and blackened. All had to be sent to the hospital for a time. A month later they were all well and out on the desert again.

There was one pitiful tragedy enacted out on those scorching sands. An airman with his mechanic went out and never returned. The Cameliers were hurried off to scour the Sahara in search of them. There had been two 'planes out. One struck engine trouble and made a forced landing. The other flew back to Kharga, after telling the pilot in the damaged machine to stay where he was till assistance arrived. Knowing—approximately—where the 'plane was stranded, the camel patrol started out. On the second day they found the tracks of the landing and the take off. The bird had flown. But not back to Kharga. Other 'planes joined in the search. Still there was no trace of the missing airmen. The weather was blazing hot—the hottest our men had ever experienced. With blistered faces and scorched hands the Cameliers kept going. If the poor pilot had only stayed where he first landed all would have been well. Water convoys moved out to replenish the meagre supplies in the fantasses. Motor-cars joined in the search. But what a tiny spot a 'plane is on thousands of square miles of desert! On the seventh day the scouts espied a white speck on the rim of the earth. They had long given up hopes of finding the airmen alive. Off they trotted and reached the 'plane. They found the pilot, Lieut. Ridley, and Mechanic Garside, both dead, but stood aghast when they saw the pilot had a bullet wound in his head. A bully-beef tin was there and a couple of biscuits. But the water had been finished days ago. Near by was a notebook, and in it Garside's diary. It told of the forced landing, the attempt to fly back, the petrol giving out, and the husbanding of the scanty water supply. Then this entry: "Lt. Ridley shot himself at 10 o'clock on Sunday morning." Death was certain for both. One might last another day or two on the water; so, to give his mechanic another faint chance to live, the young officer had gone West. "He was a very gallant gentleman."

When first the I.C.C. lobbed into Kharga they got the greatest surprise of their life. The oasis had been evacuated when the Senussi swooped down, so the Cameliers did not know whether to expect an ovation or a fusillade. So they went warily. Natives gathered round in friendly fashion, throwing the usual 'Saieeda' at the visitors, when a cheerful voice yelled out, "Hullo, Australia; what are you doing out here?" Rather nonplussed, they pulled up and looked round, but every face that wasn't brown was black as ebony. There was no sign of a white man anywhere. Then they espied a big African striding forward with a grin that exposed more teeth than Roosevelt at his fiercest.

"Who are you?" demanded the section officer.

"My name's Bluegum. I come from Kalgoorlie. I've not seen an Australian for ten years," replied the black.

It took some time to satisfy the Cameliers that old Bluegum was dinkum. "Oh, I'm an Australian all right," he said, with a laugh. "Any of you boys from the West?"

There happened to be several of the boys from Perth and Broome and the Kimberley and the Goldfields, and they crowded round old Bluegum and put the third degree on him good and hard. But he was trumps all right, and proved a very valuable ally indeed. He showed the patrol the best place to camp, where to get water and grain, and bought at very reasonable prices vegetables and fruit for the hungry and thirsty men. Probably he made a good ten or twenty per cent, for himself out of the transaction, but Maleesch! the boys didn't mind.

There was one episode in connection with the operations round Kharga and Dakla that never was mentioned in any official dispatch. Maybe it was just as well. It was not a particularly creditable episode—though a most natural one. It was midsummer, the hottest, thirstiest summer the Anzacs had ever experienced. The company had gone out after the Senussi, who were reported by aeroplane to be moving on Kharga. Orders were given to rendezvous at a certain spot called Hell's Gates, where fantasses were to be filled. One section remained behind, with orders to join up during the night. Unfortunately, or fortunately, there was no officer in charge of this section. But a canteen had been started at Kharga. And it was frightfully thirsty weather. Try as they would, the boys could not assuage their thirst. They bought bottles of whisky and put them in their saddle-bags. They mopped up unlimited beer. They waxed merry. They saw two blades of grass where one had grown before. They saw twice as many 'planes as were really on the oasis. They sang "Australia will be there." They saw two suns fiery red sinking into the west. The section sergeant returning from a visit to the outpost found his section hopeless. They loved him, and told him so. They sang to him that he was a jolly good fellow, even if there was a war on. Sergeant Blaine was something of a philosopher. He thought hard. Then he grinned and exclaimed, "Maleesch." In the midst of their cacophony he roared, "Silence. 'Saddle up'," and they saddled. Ordinarily a section of the I.C.C. can saddle up in a quarter of an hour and move off with five days' grain, water, and rations into the wilderness. In the competitions without packs or cacolets it has been done in five minutes. On this memorable occasion it took the section nearly an hour. Men were continually tripping over their gear. Several fell asleep leaning on their camels. The sun had disappeared before they were mounted. Several fell off their mounts and miraculously broke no bones. Eventually the section moved off in a column of humps, singing, "The Long, Long Trail."

The sober ones in the lead knew the track. The camels behind just naturally followed. Still more fell off, and as their camels went on they had to walk—or stagger.

Half a dozen slightly inebriated cameliers in a bunch saw, a few miles from Kharga, a camel train coming in. They yelled out, "Senussis, charge the blighters." Without waiting for orders they whipped up their patient camels, yelled like demons, and charged full tilt at the caravan. It happened to be a convoy of transport camels returning from the water-dump. The fiery cameliers were terribly disappointed.

An aeroplane passed over, flying low, for the pilot could not make out the meaning of the scene below. A scared rider cried out, "Taube," and blazed away.

Back along the track were empty bottles, full men, riderless camels, and much flotsam and jetsam. The head of the section was trotting happily to the rendezvous. At the rear came the patient sergeant coaxing the crazy ones, helping the lazy ones on with a stick.

And back at headquarters the staff were puzzled to get the following cryptic message from the aeroplane pilot: "Blaine's section last seen going for Hell's Gates, hell for leather."

Chapter 4

The Sister

This is the why and the wherefore of the coming to Egypt of Sister Flora Aird Andrews Livingstone.

A crazed Serbian killed an Austrian Archduke. This incident brought on Armageddon. It set Central Europe ablaze, and gave Germany the cue to launch out on a swashbuckling expedition with a view to making good her ambition of dominating Europe—and, incidentally, the world.

Now the Huns might have crushed France and Russia—very probably they would have done so—but the German powers that be made the unpardonable error of tearing up a scrap of paper, and ravaging Belgium with a ferocity and ruthlessness unbelievable in this twentieth century. That brought old England out of her splendid isolation, and her contemptible little army crossed the Channel, to perform such miracles against overwhelming odds that all the world wondered.

Britain having stripped for the fray, Australia simply couldn't keep out of it. Mr. Joseph Cook, the Commonwealth Prime Minister, offered 20,000 men; but this little division was to increase, until the great South Land with its insignificant population sent about 500,000 soldiers—every man a volunteer—to fight in the cause of freedom.

It was September 1914—September and springtime, when the Australian bush decks herself in all her glory. The Hunter Valley, garden of sunny New South Wales, lay like a fairer

Garden of Eden between the enveloping hills. The old river ran like a trail of silver laughter past the happy homesteads. Magpies carolled merrily, all the feathered songsters joined in the bushland melody. Golden wattle bloomed in rich profusion from the watershed to the Pacific, and filled the balmy air with the scent of honeydew. On the rich river flats, and in amongst the foot-hills, hares and paddymelons fed unmolested, while higher up the mountain rocks wallabies hopped hither and thither undisturbed by the hunters. Even the foxes and dingoes in their lairs enjoyed a period of peace, for the bush boys were already wending their way to the metropolis to embark on the great adventure. Every little farm, every homestead, every sheep and cattle station sent its quota. Sturdy youths from the towns and valleys casually remarked that they would go on a walking tour to Berlin, took train to Sydney, and enlisted in the 1st Infantry Brigade. Station lads mounted their favourite hacks, and with a cheery 'So long' took the long trail eastward to the Light Horse camp. And the heroic Australian mothers and sisters and sweethearts choked back their tears and bade them go.

Colonel Livingstone's fighting days were done. He was barely sixty years of age, but a shell in South Africa had taken off his right arm. So he lived the peaceful, prosperous life of an Australian squatter, watching his flocks and herds increase and multiply. And now that the dogs of war were again let loose he sighed to think that he had no son left to give the Empire. His only son had been killed at Eland's River, and, now a widower, all his love and ambition centred in his daughter Flora.

Barely a year had passed since she had completed her training as a nurse at Prince Alfred Hospital, and had come back to the old home to be the joy of her old father's life and the sunshine of his home. She was twenty-six years old, but looked twenty-one. Being born on the 29th of February 1888, she playfully persisted that as she had only enjoyed about half a dozen birthdays, she was really only six years old. This was her excuse for any escapade. Suitors for her hand, and incidentally for the colonel's broad acres, had come to Langlands, stayed awhile, but had not conquered. Smilingly she saw them come; sadly she watched them depart. When the Polo Carnival came to Muswellbrook, she was the most radiant figure on the ground. At the dance she was the belle of the ball. Yet ever she had remained heart-whole and happy.

Day after day the old colonel and his daughter had watched the young men, singly or in twos and threes, riding gaily along the river road that led to war and glory. From the verandah of Langlands they waved a cheery God-speed to the light-hearted volunteers. But the old man sighed and shook his head. So when the freshness of September's spring had merged into the heat of October, Flora reckoned it was time to say what had long been in her mind.

The sun had set behind the western hills, which were still sharply silhouetted against the rose-red of the afterglow. All was peaceful and quiet, save for the occasional cry of a curlew or a mopoke, or the jingle of a bullock bell down the creek. The colonel was enjoying his after-dinner cigar, and it was just at that time Flora well knew his heart was warmest and his purse-strings loosest. So she sat on the arm of his big chair and gently ruffled the few grey hairs left on his kind old head. This had been her mode of attack when she wanted a trip to the Melbourne Cup, or a late model automobile, or a new hunter, or a ball dress, and it had never yet failed her, not even when she had wanted to take up nursing in Sydney.

"Daddy," she said, nestling closer, "it must be a fine thing to give a son to fight for the King."

He thought of Eland's River, and nodded his head sadly.

"I chanced on a little verse today, Daddy. It's the most beautifully loyal verse ever written, I think. It's just the proud lament of an auld Scots wife:

*"I had three sons. I now hae nane,
I bred them toiling sairly.
But I wad gie them a' again,
To live an' dee wi' Chairlie.*

"There, isn't that fine, Daddy?" Again the colonel nodded his head. "Did you see in the *Herald* that four sons of Parson Howell-Price and the five sons of Mrs. Leane had all enlisted? I think that's just wonderful, Daddy."

"They won't all come back," said the colonel sadly.

"True; but you'd far rather have your son play the man and never return than play the craven and live at Langlands; and you'd far rather your little daughter did her bit for Australia than loaf at home living on the fat of the land."

The old man stiffened, sat bolt upright, and exclaimed, "My son I gave loyally for the Empire, though it nearly broke my heart; but not my daughter—not my daughter."

It was very late before the wilful girl won her way and the old man was induced to make the great sacrifice. But finally he capitulated. Next day Flora sent in her application for a position on the staff of one of the Australian War Hospitals. She did not get away with the first batch. That was the proud privilege of the Senior Army Nursing Sisters. Neither did she get away with the second batch. But every period of waiting has its end, so early in 1915 Sister Flora Livingstone found herself on the mail boat in Sydney harbour, looking back with tearful eyes, and waving farewell to a tall, grey-haired, one-armed old gentleman who stood on the circular quay wharf and blew his nose vigorously when anyone chanced to look in his direction.

Swinging through the heads she had a last long look at the red roofs of Mosman as the steamer breasted the waves of the blue Pacific. Sydney was left behind, then Melbourne Adelaide, and Fremantle. With no *Emden* to cause any trouble, the liner crossed the Indian Ocean, looked in at Colombo, and in the fullness of time entered the Suez Canal. On the right were Moses' Well and Sinai, and Flora was glad she had not forgotten all her Old Testament history.

Picturesque Tewfik and smellful Suez were passed, and then in turn Kubri, Kabrit, and so on to Ismailia, the one really pleasant place on the Canal. Flora saw the trenches and defences all along the Canal, waved cheerily and impartially at the Gurkhas and Indian lancers and Territorials, and cooeeed delightedly whenever she saw an Australian. With a wide expanse of desert on either side the boat steamed on past Ferdan and Kantara, and eventually anchored off Port Said.

Here the nursing Sisters disembarked, spent a while and some money in the bazaars, paying about double the value of the articles, and then took train for Cairo.

Now it so happened that just as they arrived at the main station at Cairo the 1st Australian Division was entraining for Alexandria, there to embark for Gallipoli. And as she saw that heroic band marching in platoons and battalions and brigades, the soul of Flora Livingstone was stirred as never before. They were giants, these men, tall, sun-tanned, and wiry, alert, clean-limbed, and sturdy—whole platoons averaging about six feet—whole battalions with not an undersized man amongst them. There was an English officer near her on the platform, newly arrived from France, and she almost embraced him when he said to a civilian standing by, "That's the finest body of men in the whole Allied Armies." And they were her own lads from the Sunny South. How proud she was of them! How much prouder she was to be ere a few short weeks had passed and the world resounded with their praises! And when the 1st, 2nd, 3rd, and 4th Battalions marched in—her very own brigade from sunny New South Wales—a lump came into her throat and tears streamed down her face.

The trains moved out. Discipline was relaxed. The boys seeing the Australian nurses cheered till the vast building echoed with their shouts. Unable to control her emotion,

Flora held out her arms to them and cried, "Oh, I love you; I love you all! I'll nurse you and serve you till I drop. Oh, how I love you all!"

In this wise came Sister Livingstone to Egypt, and thus she plighted her troth and swore to serve for the duration of the war—and four months afterwards.

Chapter 5

Romani—1

Romani was one of the decisive battles of the war. It settled finally the pretensions of the German-led Turks in the direction of Egypt, Prior to August 1916, the enemy had always assumed the offensive, while the British devoted their energies to the defence of the Suez Canal and Egypt. After Romani the desert campaign took on a new aspect. The British assumed the offensive. Steadily the invader was pushed back and back, till at Rafa he was driven for good and all beyond the bounds of Sinai.

The Australians in Sinai knew what thirst meant during the summer of 1916. May, June, and July had witnessed terrific heat—heat that Anglo-Egyptians of long standing declared to be the record. Soldiers in hospital at Tel el Kebir, recovering slowly from various dysenteric diseases, were stricken down by the excessive heat and died. Out east of the Canal the thirsty garrison toiled early and late, building redoubts and filling millions of sand-bags. In those enervating days there was but one joke out in the sandy waste. Said one Billjim to his mate, "What did you do in the Great War, Daddy?" And his comrade wearily replied, "I helped to bag Sinai, my boy."

The building of trenches was a hopeless task. Shovelling sand was like unto shovelling water. Fast as the sand was scooped out it trickled in again. Then, when a trench had been boarded up and wired and sand-bagged, a stifling khamseen would blow up, and the swirling sand would fall in the trenches again. The magnitude of the task can be estimated when it is remembered that during the desert campaign, which ended at Rafa, there were used 30,000,000 sand-bags, 2,000,000 square feet of timber, 50,000 rolls of wire netting, and 7000 tons of barbed wire. In addition, 220 miles of macadamised roads were constructed, 359 miles of railway, and 300 miles of water-pipes. Briefly, it was *some* job.

Romani changed all this—at least the prosaic, defensive, sit-tight part. Henceforth the defence of Egypt rested with the attacking desert column. Abdul was too busy looking west and running east to think of threatening the Canal.

Romani was preceded by two interesting interludes—the one picturesquely victorious, the other even more picturesque, but quite a regrettable incident. At Duiedar the Scotties held an outpost. In the dark the Turks crept up, and at dawn attacked in greatly superior force. But the Scotties fought magnificently, and in spite of many casualties beat off their assailants, and held the line till the Anzac Mounted came up and drove off the enemy. The other interlude was the surprising of some Yeomanry who were routed and sent in full retreat to Kantara, where one breathless officer arrived in his pyjamas!

After that, the Cavalry and Camelry and Light Horse and Mounted Rifles patrolled the front unceasingly, while the airmen did a daily reconnaissance. The movements of the enemy were thus carefully noted and the element of surprise eliminated. So we knew in July that a considerable force of Turks was making steadily towards Romani. We did not know, however, how perfect had been the preparations of the German Staff, how rough roads had been constructed over the soft sand for the passage of artillery, how ammunition and stores had been sent ahead and hidden in the palm groves; how plans of all our defences had been made from photos by German airmen, and how old wells all along the old caravan route had been reopened and put in working order. Their telephonic signal communications were perfect. It is doubtful, however, if the Hun really thought he could break through to Kantara. The most he could hope for was to make a big feint for Egypt, and so keep as many British troops as possible in Sinai and prevent their being sent to France.

During July the enemy arrangements were completed, and in August he advanced to the attack. Patrols of the 1st Light Horse Brigade met the Turkish patrols, and on 3rd August this brigade found itself opposing the determined attack of the main army. Brigadier-General Meredith therefore threw his regiments right in the path of the invader, blocking his advance and forcing him to deploy. The superior mobility of the Australians enabled them to choose excellent positions from which to fight rear-guard actions, and while they inflicted considerable losses on the enemy, they got off very lightly. Thus the enemy was enticed into the maze of sand-dunes, where his heavily laden infantry floundered and had all the ginger taken out of their attack. Still, by sheer force of numbers the Turks won through on to Mount Meredith, Wellington Ridge, and Mount Royston.

By daylight on 4th August the 2nd Light Horse Brigade, with Brigadier-General Royston in temporary command, swung up to the battle line, and the two brigades, fighting side by side, continued to hold up the advance. But the Turkish infantry were now helped very materially by German gunners and machine gunners. Their artillery was splendidly served, shell after shell exploding over the ridges lined by the defenders, or in the wadis where the led horses were waiting. The Taubes participated in the attack, spotting for their artillery, bombing our horses and trenches, and then flying back to a specially prepared landing-place a few miles east and taking on more bombs for our annoyance. Our airmen on inferior machines did heroic stunts, but admitted themselves hopelessly out-manoeuvred and out-flown.

On our left flank towards Muhamediya the Scottish infantry barred the way. Knowing the ranges, they were able to inflict considerable damage on the Turks. Enjoying the comparative security of trenches with formidable barbed wire entanglements in front, Abdul could not get near them, and their losses were slight.

Down south the Queenslanders effectually blocked any out-flanking of our right wing. The Fighting Fifth had a very strenuous time. It was just such a fight as poor Colonel Hubert Harris—who was killed on Gallipoli—would have loved. But Lieut.-Colonel Wilson handled the Fifth with consummate skill. A few thousand Turks swinging round to attack Romani from the south found only a regiment of Light Horse in their way. But these bushmen were ubiquitous. Everywhere that Abdul went the Fifth were sure to go. Always there was a fringe of emu plumes on the crest of every hill. The superior numbers of the enemy availed him not. His casualties increased every hour, but his goal ever receded.

The boys of the Australian Light Horse have a wonderful admiration for General Royston. He is essentially a cavalry general, like Jeb Stewart. He has been fighting Zulus or Boers or Huns ever since his sixteenth year. He commanded Australians in South Africa. Coming to Sinai, he commanded first the 12th A.L.H. Regiment, then the 2nd Brigade, and finally the 3rd Light Horse Brigade, and always the men loved him for his fighting fearlessness. At Romani he was a ball of inexhaustible energy. One after another his horses knocked up, but he seemed to be made of greenhide and whalebone. And he bore a charmed life. Bullets and shrapnel fell thick and fast all round him. His A.D.C. and several orderlies were wounded, but Fighting Jack galloped on unscathed—always where the fighting was thickest.

The New Zealand Mounted Rifles, a brigade of Yeomanry, and a brigade of Territorial Infantry now came into the fight. The sorely-tried Light Horsemen had been hard at it for nearly forty-eight hours without a spell. Their horses were knocked up and starving. The men were hard put to it to keep awake. They had fought a wonderful rear-guard action, holding up and inflicting heavy casualties on an enemy five times their strength, and taking all the sting out of the offensive. But still the German Staff persevered with the attack. On came the Turks, yelling, "Allah finish Australia, Allah finish Australia"—a rather unique battle-cry, which tickled the Anzacs immensely.

From the Scottish redoubts on the left to the camelry on the right the action now became general. The Turks pushed on till their vanguard was right in sight of Romani. Here near ancient Pelusium, where the Persian hosts of Cambyses routed the Egyptians centuries before, another invader was to meet with a far different fate. But as the Turkish vanguard pushed along the wadi towards the railway no one dared prophesy what would happen. The German guns having the range to a yard, fired a never-ending hail of shrapnel on our front line, our horse lines, and on the redoubts. They had tons of ammunition. The Light Horse captured a whole camel train of ammunition, but this never affected the enemy's fire. Our artillery? having less definite objects to concentrate on and with constantly varying ranges, yet did splendid work. The Ayrshire battery in particular won the whole-souled admiration of the Anzacs. Every time a likely target showed up the Lowlanders smashed it instantly. Once some German machine guns, cleverly posted, were inflicting considerable damage on the Australians. The Ayrshires vouchsafed the Huns three shells, which landed precisely on the spot, wrecking the guns and slaughtering the teams. One silent and twisted gun barrel sticking in the air told the tale. Anon a camel team bringing up ammunition was sighted. A few shells were sent in their direction, and after the dust had subsided an Australian in a pained voice expostulated to the gunner, "Look, Scottie, there's *one* of them camels making off home."

Chapter 6

Romani—2

The battle waged with increased vigour all along the line, Romani in the centre being the main objective. It was at Romani that the Turks made their final thrust. Along the wadi, out of sight of the gunners, came an irresistible wedge of Turkish infantry. It was a spear thrust right at the heart of our position. For a while it threatened seriously. No thin line of khaki horsemen could block that rush. Abdul had staked his all on one desperate charge.

That rush might have won the day but for the New Zealanders. As the Turks came on, yelling, "Allah finish Australia," the Mounted Rifles saw their chance. With a blood-curdling yell the Maorilanders charged with the bayonet, and cut their way clean through the attacking column, cleaving it in two. Auckland, Canterbury, Wellington, and Otago won the day The head was sawn off the spear. The Turkish column, bisected neatly, faltered, and the rear half retreated. Had the first half possessed a clever leader, had they any zest for the fight, they might have made things merry.

But just as they realised they were cut off, the New Zealanders were upon them with the bayonet, yelling like demons. Nothing could withstand that charge. The Turks dropped their rifles and called for quarter. The victorious "Allah finish Australia" died on their lips, and they and their German officers cried "Kamerad," "Finish war," "Australia good." In the vicinity of Mount Royston the New Zealanders bagged 500 prisoners.

As the enemy wavered the British line advanced. Round Katib Gannit there was some stiff fighting, till the Light Horsemen manoeuvred the Turks into a hopeless position. Rifle and machine-gun fire concentrated on them, and when the Light Horse charged 400 Turks surrendered.

Round about Romani were performed many deeds of valour that some chronicler may perhaps redeem from oblivion. One heroic incident stands out because of the peculiar circumstances connected therewith. During April and May, when the Australian infantry left Egypt for France, quite a number of Light Horsemen, hearing 'the call of Stoush,' and thinking that Sinai would not provide them with sufficient excitement, stowed away on the transports and mingled with the infantry. Several managed to elude the vigilance of the Military Police at Marseilles and got right up to the front line, where in due course the majority of them were killed or wounded. Several, however, were caught on the transports or at Marseilles; and in time were returned crestfallen to Egypt. Amongst these was Curran of the 7th A.L.H. Technically he had deserted, so he was placed under arrest. And he was under arrest when Abdul swooped down on Romani. It was against his nature to miss a scrap, but his rifle had been taken from him. So he escaped from the guard and started out on his own as a stretcher-bearer. Right out to the front line he went, entirely indifferent to the death-dealing hail that spattered in the sand. Slightly wounded men he gave water to drink, and cheered them on their way in with jest and joke. The badly wounded he helped or carried in himself. Fourteen times he braved the bullets, and each time brought in a wounded man. But his good luck petered out. When next he essayed to carry out his errand of mercy, he was killed. He had shown the 'greater love.' He had laid down his life not only for his country but for his friends.

Romani was now fought and won. Scottish and English Territorials, Australian and New Zealand horsemen, cavalry and camelry, now pushed on to complete the overthrow of the enemy. The German gunners, so accurate at known ranges, lost their sting as the British line swept forward. They shortened their range again and again till it was time to make a getaway. The machine gunners tried in vain to hold up the pursuit. Parties of Turkish infantry, tired out and dispirited with their long march, their incessant fighting, and their final defeat, surrendered all along the line. About 20,000 with several guns and a big quota of machine guns had started out from El Arish. About 18,000 had come into action between Katia and Romani. Of these, by the time the pursuit was finally held up, 5000 were captured; over 1200 were killed; about 4500 had been wounded. In honour of their 'Victory'(?) the Turks struck a Romani medal.

The Anzac Mounted Division enjoyed a brief rest for the sake of their horses, and the pursuit was resumed. Yeomanry and camelry co-operated in the hunt. The 3rd Light Horse Brigade, having accounted for an isolated body of the enemy to the southward, made a belated arrival on the scene, and joined in the chase. But round about Katia the defeated Turks were rallied. Strong rear-guards with many machine guns were thrown across the line of our advance. In spite of gallant attacks and splendid charges on to adventurous rear-parties, the Turks would no longer be thrown into disorder. The rear-guard was harried, but the main body was not hurried. Every inch of the way back was fiercely contested. After a few days of hard righting the pursuit eased up, and Abdul marched back to Bir el Abd.

Romani is claimed to be largely an Anzac victory, for the Anzac Mounted Division, under General Chauvel, bore the brunt of the attack, and had almost a monopoly of the casualties. Of the total casualties the Yeomanry had 2 per cent., the British infantry and artillery 10 per cent., and the Anzacs 87 per cent.

Amongst the 5000 prisoners captured were a number of German officers and men. One of these officers was talking to a group of Australian Light Horse officers when a long and wiry trooper, with characteristic disregard for the conventions, butted in and exclaimed, "Say, old Hun, what do you think of the Australians now?"

And the German officer replied, "They are splendid fighters. Still, I do not think they are any better than they think they are." Which, all things considered, was one to the Hun.

That trooper's ruffled feelings were, however, mollified when he read in the English papers Mr. W. T. Massey's tribute that the Anzac Mounted Division was the cream of the Overseas Forces.

CHAPTER 7

The Soldier

Some day the war historians will get busy over the Sinai Campaign. For difficulties encountered and hardships endured, it must rank as one of the most interesting campaigns ever carried to a successful issue.

From the first skirmishes east of the Canal—not, of course, including the original abortive attacks of the Turks at the beginning of 1915—to the capture of Rafa, the bulk of the patrols and the brunt of the fighting fell on the Anzacs. Yet it was not till well into 1917 that the people of Australia realised what a heroic part had been played in that campaign by the Australian Light Horse, New Zealand Mounted Rifles, and Imperial Camel Corps. Owing to some oversight of the Commonwealth Government, no Australian Press representative had been detailed for the task of informing Australian fathers and mothers how heroically their sons had fought and died.

Thus day after day, when the mails arrived from the Antipodes, sun-scorched troopers out on the desert or wounded men in hospital were sickened by letters from their loved ones saying, "We never hear anything about the Light Horse," or, "You're lucky you're not in France," or, "I suppose you hardly know there's a war on there." The climax came when a badly-wounded Light Horseman in the 14th Australian General Hospital received a pair of socks from the Red Cross. Inside was a message from some well-meaning but very cruel young lady, and the message read: "I hope these sox go to some Australian hero in France, but not to any of the cold-footed Light Horse." That trooper cried like a kid.

In 1916 the G.O.C., A.I.F., in Egypt and Sinai, General Sir Harry Chauvel, seeing the totally inadequate reports of the battles which were being cabled out to Australia, cabled to the Defence Department, recommending that a war correspondent be sent to keep the people in touch with operations in Sinai, and to compile the war records of the A.I.F. regiments. But for some inscrutable reason nothing was done.

So the meagre reports of the doings of the Light Horsemen continued to percolate through the home papers and the cables to Australia. Romani was billed as a great British victory in which, incidentally, the Australians and New Zealanders participated. But in 1917 a paragraph in the Sydney *Bulletin* told astonished readers that during the fighting round Katia and Romani the Anzacs had suffered over 87 per cent, of the total casualties. The published reports of the battle, and the subsequent rewards and decorations, never gave a hint of such disproportionate losses. If the Light Horse did any particularly good work, the cables in the English papers—zealously copied and condensed for Australian consumption—referred to "Our Mounted Troops" or "The Victorious Desert Column." And later on, at the second battle of Gaza, when the Imperial Camel Corps (1st Anzac Battalion) was the only unit to reach its objective and capture the Turkish redoubts, the cables told Australian readers that "The Camel Corps did good work carrying water for the Light Horse."

There are lone graves left on the league-long track from Romani to El Arish. Day after day the Light Horse and Camel patrols pushed eastward, ever eastward. Every now and then there were skirmishes with the Turkish patrols, and Abdul is no slouch as a scout and sniper. And following the track blazed by the Anzacs came the British infantry and the pipe line and the iron horse. There was heavy fighting round the Katia Oasis, amongst the palms, for the German Staff had selected the rearguard halting-places with consummate skill, and the Light Horse being the attacking party suffered many casualties. The Turkish defence of the Katia line was so stubborn and so successful that the main Turkish army, which fled in disorder from Romani, was able to continue the retreat to El Arish in comparative ease. There is a fine story waiting to be written by some New Zealander who was with the Mounted Rifles during the strenuous months from June 1916 to January 1917. English Staff officers, competent critics, have declared that the New Zealanders were the pick of the whole E.E.F., and I've heard Australians gladly endorse that verdict. Australians and New Zealanders fought side by side all the time, and as the scorching heat of summer gave place to the bitter cold of winter, they pushed steadily on, always in the van. ... On the occasion of the second trek to Palestine of the 1st Anzac Battalion I.C.C., I saw three graves on the scrubby sand-hills near Bir el Abd. They were not very far apart. Rough wooden crosses marked the sites. I rode across to investigate, for I had many Light Horsemen comrades killed in Sinai. These, however, proved to be three troopers of the Otago Mounted Rifles—Ryan, Mahoney, and M'Carthy; three gallant Irish-Colonial crusaders.

After suffering a fair share of casualties at Romani, the Cameliers moved eastward with the Desert Column. Day after day the patrols pushed on, and the railway construction followed apace. The Hun 'planes kept busy bombing the Desert Column and the dumps and the railway. Our 'planes went up daily, and had fine sport with enemy fliers. Whatever there is sporting or chivalrous in the German army seems to have risen to the Flying Corps. Dare-devil Hun airmen, after bombing the Light Horse bivouacs and the railhead workers, dropped cheeky messages on the Australians. At this period the bombing of our dumps and working parties was a regular occurrence. 'Archies' being rather scarce, the only thing to do was to dive for a dugout. On one occasion a Light Horseman was watching a gang of E.L.C. natives at work, when they suddenly downed tools and dashed for a big trench near which he was standing. Intuitively the trooper guessed there was a Taube above, so he dived for the trench, landing a half-second ahead of the gyppies, who piled themselves on top of him. As the last native landed in the trench there was a deafening explosion and a wild chorus of yells. The lucky horseman scrambled from underneath the writhing mass without a scratch, but several of the gyppies were badly wounded and a few killed outright. Familiarity with bombs bred contempt, and soon the sight of dozens of men streaking for the shelter of a dugout provoked naught but a mild interest or simple mirth.

One incident provided the comic relief which kept railhead laughing for a week. An A.S.C. officer was superintending the stacking of some *dhurra*, incidentally yarning with an Australian and at the same time keeping one eye on a black dot in the sky overhead. Suddenly there was a warning whistle, and the pair dived for the shelter of a dugout, making a dead heat of it, while the Australian's dog came third. Hardly were they settled before there was a sound of scrambling, and a frightened native, being too far from his own dugout, and risking anything rather than remain in the open, flung himself headlong into the dugout. The sagacious dog resenting this intrusion, snapped at the native, nipping him painfully on the fleshiest part of his body. But at the precise instant the dog bit, the aeroplane bomb exploded, and the poor gyppie, thinking he was mortally wounded, grabbed the injured part and ran howling to the Field Ambulance.

Time came when railhead and pipehead and roadhead had been pushed far enough eastward for the G.O.C. to reckon he was within striking distance of El Arish—and El Arish is the half-way house to Jerusalem. For several days the enemy 'planes had been over reconnoitring and bombing, so when all was ready for the final dash on El Arish, our 'planes were kept very busy keeping the enemy airmen away.

For long the Turks had made El Arish their base for operations against Egypt. Its strategical advantages were many. Surrounded by a natural barrier in the shape of rolling billows of sand, the approach of attacking forces was made very difficult. It looked absolutely impassable for artillery; yet our guns got through. With its hills and palm groves it might have been stubbornly defended, but at the last moment the German Staff, having a wholesome respect for the encircling manoeuvres of the Desert Column, decided on evacuation. So just when the British were about to strike, the airmen came in with the news that the Turks were leaving. It was therefore decided to send the camelry and cavalry on ahead to make sure, and to capture the town. So on top of a hard day's march the Desert Column moved off again at midnight for El Arish. Over the sand-dunes they trekked, a moving mass of mounted men—but silently, and with no tell-tale pipes or cigarettes to warn Abdul of their approach. Masaid, a few miles west of El Arish, had been strongly entrenched and held, but the advance guard found here only empty trenches. On went the column over precipitous sand-banks, so steep that one wondered how the camels and horses didn't topple over. When nearing the town just at dawn, the column divided and surrounded the town on the west, south, and east sides—to the north being the blue Mediterranean. But the bird had flown.

The ancient town with its mosque and mud-built houses was all astir. For over two years the Turks had held sway there. But when the Light Horsemen cantered into view, the Bedouins came out to greet them. And they showed as much jubilation as a Bedouin ever shows—which is not a great deal. So the main army followed on, horse, foot, artillery, and camelry, and camped beneath the palms on the banks of the Wadi el Arish. They rested. But the hard-worked Desert Column had a very brief respite. Hardly had they settled in their new bivouac before they were once more hurried off to mop up Maghdaba.

Chapter 8

The Soldier

The battle of Maghdaba was one of the most brilliant and picturesque little battles in the whole war. It was rather presumptuous of the Anzac Mounted Division to think that it could manage the job.

On the face of it, no student of war would believe that a small body of dismounted cavalry and camelry, armed only with rifle and bayonet, could charge across open country and capture a strong natural fortress, heavily entrenched, defended by a resolute soldiery scarcely inferior in strength, and armed with artillery, machine guns, and bombs. And this on the top of a 20-mile night march over unknown country. Yet that is exactly what the Anzacs did.

The Turks having found discretion the better part of valour, retired eastward from El Arish, leaving the half-way house to Palestine to the British.

But blocking the further progress of our army towards Sinai were the two strongly entrenched and well-garrisoned posts of Rafa and Maghdaba, and because of the absence of water on the way and the difficulty of transport the Turks felt fairly secure at Maghdaba.

After an all-night trek down the Wadi el Arish, the Anzac Mounted Division, plus the Cameliers, came at dawn in sight of Maghdaba. It was a weird and wonderful stunt, that march in the silent stillness of the night. Like a column of spectres the Cameliers glided noiselessly down the wadi bed. Now and then, however, from the ranks of the Light Horsemen came the clang of a stirrup iron or the clink of snaffle bars. Riding near the Bing Boys one could see against their swarthy faces the gleam of white teeth or the sparkle of black eyes. Not a light was shown. There was no smoking. It is a terrible act of self-denial for the Australian to go without a smoke for any length of time. It was a long, slow, sleepy, silent ride. Abdul therefore got the surprise of his life when, with the breaking day, the Light Horse patrols came circling round his stronghold.

There was hurry and hustle and excitement, then, amongst the men of Maghdaba. The supports were hurriedly thrown into the trenches and redoubts. The guns behind the hills were mounted, and soon their shells began to play upon the manoeuvring horsemen. The 6th Light Horse came under a salvo of shrapnel. It looked as if dozens of saddles must be emptied, but not a man was hit. The regiment manoeuvred as on parade, and swung clear of the danger-zone. The Cameliers—three companies of Australians and one of New Zealanders—dismounted out of artillery range, and in a long drab line moved forward gaily to the attack. On the right the 2nd Light Horse Brigade swung up, dismounted, and, while the horses moved back to safety, the troopers joined up with the Cameliers and pressed on. The enemy artillery, Krupp and mountain guns, having kept the horses at a distance, now concentrated on the long line of approaching riflemen. Knowing the ranges, they made good practice, but the continually moving line necessitated a shortening range, and the fire was not very deadly.

The Bing Boys (Hong-Kong and Singapore Mountain Battery) now took a hand. In double-quick time they barracked their camels, put their mountain guns together, and quickly finding the range, devoted their attention to the Turkish redoubts. Our Royal Horse Artillery next took up the running, and from behind a convenient rise engaged in some counter battery work at the expense of the Turkish gunners. The action became general, and the fusillade of musketry all along the line was punctuated by the roar of the artillery. Nearer and nearer crept the long khaki line to the Turkish redoubts, and a steady contest began for the desired superiority of fire. The enemy machine guns were well served, but on the whole their musketry was very second rate.

Word of the dash on Maghdaba had reached the enemy headquarters, and a strong mounted force was sent to relieve the garrison. But the New Zealanders swung round to the north-east, held up the relief, and, attacking vigorously, sent them back in disorder to the frontier. Maghdaba was now almost surrounded, but the advantage of position lay with the defenders. They were all under cover in excellently prepared trenches, while the Anzacs were attacking in the open. But the latter's marksmanship at long ranges was far superior. The crests of the redoubts were lashed with bullets, so that the Turks feared to raise their heads, and their fire grew erratic. Nearer and nearer drew the attacking force. Hotter and hotter grew the fire. Horsemen, Yeomanry, and Cameliers, now fired with the spirit of emulation, made a race of it. Soon they were within striking distance of the enemy. A rattle ran along the line, and a glint of steel shimmering in the sun told Abdul that the bayonets were out. A cheer sounded, and was carried from end to end of the line. The whistles sounded the 'Charge,' and the attackers sprang forward. Faster sounded the Turkish fire, but it was wild, mostly whistling harmlessly overhead. The British never troubled any longer to reply. The bayonet was to settle the whole matter. The line now broke up as the cheering soldiery faced straight at the various redoubts. There was a wild final charge, some hot work with the bayonet, and soon white flags began to show up in the redoubts. One after another the scattered post garrisons surrendered. Each redoubt was, however, commanded by the one farther on. But the day was already won. Small parties of Turks were flying in all directions, and wild-eyed Anzacs, too tired to chase them, swore lustily and blazed away a few parting shots. Away east, Yeomanry and Mounted Rifles were rounding up the fugitives, and only a few hundred got away. The last redoubt was captured, and the victors charged for the German guns and finished the fight.

Back on the plain were dozens of still khaki figures. Here and there were stretcher-bearers carrying in the wounded. At the dressing-stations the doctors and medical orderlies were working furiously. Parties were told off to bury the dead. Our losses, considering the lack of cover during the attack, were surprisingly few. Five officers had been killed and 17 wounded. Seven other ranks were killed and 117 wounded.

It was at this stage, while all hands were busy bringing in the prisoners and the wounded, that one camel went mangoon. Breaking away from the line and tearing the nose-peg free, it started out to mop up the earth. Every Camelier that crossed its path had to flee for his life. Huge stones were hurled at the brute, but it grew madder and madder, and nothing could stop it. Then the Camelier Medico sauntered into view, and the enraged beast charged fair at him. There were wild yells of warning, and the Doc made the run of his life. He turned and doubled round and about, dodging like a tricky rugby three-quarter, but the camel, ignoring all others, followed hard in his wake. The crowd divided their time between cheering on the Doc and heaving bricks at the camel. At last the medico saw in a heap of forage a haven of rest. The Cameliers were now taking pot-shots at the camel, which, bleeding from half a dozen wounds, still floundered at the heels of its quarry. Then to the surprise of all and the intense relief of the Doctor, the camel stopped, and started feeding away at the *dhurra*.

The Maghdaba garrison was wiped out. Comparatively few escaped. Over 1300 prisoners were bagged, including 45 officers. Four mountain guns and three Krupp guns, with a big store of ammunition, rifles, and machine guns, were gathered in. And when these were got ready the victorious cavalcade started off back to El Arish. More reinforcements appeared out East, but the Light Horse shepherded the column home, and the Turks dared not attack.

Chapter 9

The Sister

It was night. All the lights in B4 were out except the shaded globe on Sister's table. All was quiet save when, now and then, some weary soldier groaned, or maybe fighting his battles over again in his sleep, gave forth some incoherent ejaculation.

Without, the full Egyptian moon shed a silvery light on old Cairo and the Nile, while the age-old Mokattam Hills loomed black and Sphinx-like to eastward. A gentle breeze filtered through the windows. Sister Livingstone sat at the table. It was her turn for night duty, and, having seen all her patients comfortably settled for the night, she was revelling in the newly arrived Australian mail. Strange how welcome the most trivial home news becomes when one is in a far country. How the soldiers, and the Sisters too, just long for news from home.

Sister had finished reading her mail, and now, staring into space, was thinking dreamily of sunny New South Wales and the old homestead in the Hunter River Valley. She was thinking of old times—the dances, the polo carnivals, the shooting excursions in the mountains, and the picnic races.

Suddenly she was roused from her reverie. In the distance there sounded a long, tremulous note rising high and shrill, then dying away to a soft, plaintive cry. It was the cry of the curlew, that sad, mournful bush note that no Australian, once hearing, ever forgets.

Again the cry was repeated, nearer it seemed, yet so softly that she seemed to hear but the echo of it.

Rising softly she tiptoed towards the door. Passing No. 7 bed an aggrieved voice in a stage whisper cried, "O' course I don't want any attention at all. I'm only a silkworm."

"What's up, Billjim, old chap?" said Sister, going to his side.

"Oh, nothing at all; just dying o'thirst."

Smiling, Sister brought 'him a drink, and when she had turned and smoothed his pillow, he looked up with a grin and said, "O'course you don't want to kiss me goodnight, Sister."

"Oh, I daren't, Billjim; the rest of the Australian Eleven would be jealous."

"But I wouldn't tell. What sort of a nark do you take me for?"

"Walls have ears," she replied sententiously, "and the night has a thousand eyes."

Glancing round the ward to see that all was well, Sister again moved towards the door, and looked forth into the night. She was still wondering whence came the cry of the curlew, when she saw a beckoning hand at the end of the verandah. It was Blaine, the big sergeant, who always slept in the open. Born and bred in the bush, he said the walls of houses and hospitals seemed to cramp and stifle him. He was smiling as Sister came up. She expostulated gently, "It's nearly midnight, and time you were asleep."

"You promised to write home to poor Mrs. Giltinan tonight, Sister, and I promised to tell you why George died."

"Why he died?" she reiterated in a surprised voice.

"Well, how he died."

"Very well," she acquiesced, seating herself at the bedside. "I'm afraid I was dreaming when I heard that curlew. It brought such a flood of bushland memories with it. But I didn't know there were any curlews about here."

"There aren't," said the soldier, with a grin.

"What, you did it?"

"Well, you see, Sister, I peeped through the window, and you looked so awfully sweet with the light shining on your pretty angel face that I simply had to bring you out to make sure if you really were an angel."

"'It's a lee, but it's a bonnie, bonnie lee,'" she quoted.

"Oh, you've been reading J. M. Barrie," he said.

Sister nodded, and was silent for a while.

"On such a night as this, a couple of thousand years ago," he said quietly, "Antony and Cleopatra glided down this same old Nile, with the same moon floating aloft, and the same old pyramids standing sentinel."

"Suppose you tell me about Giltinan instead of Cleopatra," Sister suggested.

"Righto," said the patient, pocketing the gentle rebuke. "But mind I can only give the facts. You will have to decide how much or how little you will tell poor George's mother."

Sister nodded, and Robert Blaine proceeded:

"George Giltinan was one of the very best lads in my troop, and perhaps the crack shot of the 7th Light Horse. At the range, once he'd got his sighters right, he frequently registered a possible, and you could safely back him to get a three-inch group at 200. One day we were out on the Petrified Forest and he winged a hawk at 900 yards. But the most wonderful thing was that at night-time he was a deadly shot. Well, you know that on Gallipoli the Turkish trenches were anything from 10 yards to 100 yards from ours, except on the flat opposite Gaba Tepe. Here the Navy dominated the position, and there was a stretch of no-man's-land about 1000 yards wide. We patrolled this area every night, and had some exciting skirmishes with the Turkish patrols. Now one night I had a dozen men out. We were about 500 yards in front, and Giltinan was with me. He was a fine fellow, as hefty a lad as you could want for a rough and tumble, a great footballer, and as strong as a horse. 'Birdie' wanted a prisoner, and we were dead set on getting one. Now just a little after midnight we were lying doggo, when I saw, dimly outlined ahead, a short, stout figure with a forage cap on. It could be nothing else but a Turk, yet there was something curiously familiar about it. I heard a movement on my left, and cried out as loudly as I dared, 'Don't shoot, George;' but it was too late. Even as I spoke his rifle went off, and the figure in front, with a cry that rings in my ears even now, threw up his arms and fell."

"Who was it?" asked Sister.

"Well, Giltinan thought it was a Turk—so did we all, but I couldn't get over the feeling that it was someone that I knew. So, taking George and another chap with me, I went forward to investigate. We had gone about 30 yards when I heard a voice say, 'That you, Bob?' It was poor Captain Wood, lying on his back with a bullet wound in his chest. He had evidently been doing some reconnaissance on his own. As I bent over him he gasped, 'Better leave me, Blaine, old chap. I think I'm a goner. Go on. Imshee.'

"'Oh, you're worth a dozen dead men yet,' I answered to reassure him; but his face was deathly white, and I feared he spoke truly. Giltinan never spoke once while we carried the captain in. The latter just remarked, 'Bit of bad luck, wasn't it? Maleesch.' The M.O. bound up his wound, and reported to the colonel that poor Wood could hardly survive the night. I went into the dressing-station to see him before turning in. 'Good-bye, Bob, old chap. Don't tell me who fired, but he was a d——d good shot, wasn't he?' So they carried him down to the beach and off to the hospital ship *Gascon*. A week later we heard that he was dead."

"Cruel luck," murmured Sister.

"Poor Giltinan never spoke to a soul for a week. All the boys wondered what had come over him. Only a couple of us knew. He volunteered for all the dare-devil patrols. When there was a stunt on he exposed himself recklessly. He seemed just itching to get killed, but, as often happens with men who are tired of living, he bore a charmed life. He got two bullets through his tunic, yet himself went scathless. One night he was out fixing barbed wire, and a machine gun opened and put a few shots round him, and one pierced his hat. 'You're a rotten shot,' he cried in derision to Abdul, then sauntered back over the parapet. He grew thin and gaunt and haggard. The Doc asked him if he was sick, and he replied that he was better than he was ever likely to be again. Some of our non-com.'s were killed and wounded, and the troop officer wanted to make Giltinan a corporal, but he said he had enough stripes on his conscience without having any on his arm.

"One night I was asleep, and Giltinan was in the next dug-out. Suddenly I was awakened by him rushing into my 'possie' wild-eyed and dishevelled. 'Listen,' he cried fiercely.

"'Rat-at-tat, tat, rat-at-tat.'

"'Why,' I laughed, 'that's only Abdul with his machine gun. He's been at it every night for weeks and we can't locate him.'

"'Yes, but hark what he's saying,' persisted the wild-eyed warrior.

"Once again there sounded the familiar barking of the maxim, 'Rat-at-tat, tat, rat-at-tat.'

"'There,' he demanded; 'did you get it that time? "Giltinan is a guilty man. Giltinan is a guilty man." That thing has been haunting me days and nights for months, and I can't stand it any longer.'

"I tried to laugh away his fears, but he was obdurate. At last I seemed to share his hallucination, and it appeared that the maxim was ticking out, 'Giltinan is a guilty man.' At last poor George could bear it no longer. 'I won't stand it,' he cried, and rushed out into the night.

"I feared for his reason, so, slipping into my boots, I followed fast after him. There was a bit of a moon, and I could just see him grab his rifle and rush up the communication trench to the front line. When I reached the fire trench I saw him standing on the parapet and blazing away in the direction of the maddening maxim.

"'Come down, Giltinan,' I roared. But he only laughed the wild laugh of a maniac, and ramming another five cartridges into his magazine he once more blazed away. The Turkish trenches opposite were soon spitting, fire and bullets began to zip all round him.

"At last the boys couldn't stand it. Someone shouted, 'Grab him.' Four of us made for the parapet, but before we could clamber over, a commanding voice cried, 'Stop.' It was Major Cameron. 'I can't risk four good men over one madman,' and I suppose he was right.

"The whole Turkish fine was now blazing away at Giltinan, who was firing and laughing and yelling like mad. It was a miracle how he escaped. We yelled at him to come back, and our line opened fire to counteract to some extent the Turkish fusillade. But it couldn't last. The wild laugh on Giltinan's lips suddenly changed to a choking gasp, and he fell back into our trench.

"The next day we buried him, and—such is the irony of fate—a few hours later we received word that Captain Wood was not dead, but out of danger and doing well in the hospital at Alexandria."

CHAPTER 10

The Soldier

In the days of trench warfare, when battles last for weeks and months, it is pleasant to dwell on battles like Romani and Maghdaba, for they only lasted a few hours. There was no long-drawn-out agony of stalemate, and there was no doubt as to who won. As the Australians expressed it, 'they were dinkum scraps.'

Another victory, sudden, brilliant, and decisive, which history must place to the credit of Sir Harry Chauvel and the victorious Desert Column, was that at Rafa. After their splendid fight at Maghdaba, they returned for a brief respite at El Arish, then made a sudden dash on Rafa. The fight was fiercely contested—the Turks in their well-fortified stronghold, the British on the open desert—but as at Maghdaba the victorious Desert Column performed wonders. The entire Turkish garrison was killed, wounded, or carried off in triumph to El Arish.

Rafa is on the extreme north-east corner of Sinai, just within the Egyptian boundary, and therefore just on the border of Palestine. It was the last Turkish stronghold on the eastern frontier, and as it was only about 30 miles from El Arish, it constituted a menace to the Egyptian outpost, so Sir Archibald Murray decided to treat it to the same medicine that had been meted out to Maghdaba.

Marching out of El Arish on the evening of 8th January, the Desert Column's striking force was composed of a portion of the Anzac Mounted Division, some companies of the Imperial Camel Corps, some Yeomanry, British Territorial Artillery, the Hong-Kong and Singapore Mountain Battery, and aeroplanes. The bulk of the force consisted of Anzacs, and their performance justified the title conferred on them after Romani as the "Cream of the Overseas Forces."

The enemy made the same mistake that they made at Maghdaba. They thought it impossible for a mobile force strong enough to attack Rafa to move up from El Arish before Turkish reinforcements could arrive. Yet the Flying Column did a 30-mile night march over the desert, and within twenty-four hours had the battle fought and won. Turkish relieving columns were hurried up from Shellal and Khan Yunis, in all nearly 4000 strong, but the New Zealanders held them off till the stronghold was captured and the remnant of the garrison safely on the road to El Arish. The only effect of the abortive attempt to relieve Rafa was to encourage the garrison to a fiercer resistance, and so add to the toll of their casualties.

Leaving El Arish at four o'clock on the afternoon of 8th January, the Desert Column reached Sheikh Zoweid in five hours, and bivouacked till half-past one in the morning. The moonlight march was then resumed, and by dawn our patrols had come into touch with the enemy at Magruntain. Here the main Turkish force was entrenched, the site being a couple of miles from Rafa. German engineers and gunners had worked zealously to make the stronghold impregnable. There were several lines of trenches. In odd vantage posts were cleverly concealed rifle-pits. Posted round the central position were six large, well-constructed redoubts. Krupp mountain guns and well-trained German machine gunners afforded additional strength to the Turkish regulars who constituted the garrison. To add to the difficulties of the British the attack had to be made in the open, our ground lacking any cover whatever. As the attackers were operating 30 miles from their base, the Turks—like they did at Maghdaba—thought they could beat off all attacks till lack of supplies, shells, and especially water, compelled the Desert Column to swing back, disgruntled and discouraged, on El Arish. Once again the Turks miscalculated the quality of the Anzacs and the punch of the Camelry.

The defences of Rafa were so constructed as to withstand attack from all quarters; and this was well, for the attack came from all sides at once. In the dim light of dawn the garrison could be seen hurrying and scurrying in all directions, proof positive that the rapid advance of the British had taken them unawares. Having captured and isolated an Arab encampment five miles to the southward, the New Zealanders pushed on and captured the town of Rafa. This done, they swung round and attacked the Magruntain position from the rear.

This manoeuvre cut the Turks off from Palestine, prevented any reinforcement reaching them, and blocked their retreat. The British artillery then, aided and abetted by the aerial scouts, pounded away at the Turkish redoubts, and engaged in a duel with the German gunners. Under cover of a very strenuous bombardment the attack developed, and was pushed home with the utmost gallantry.

Companies of the 1st (Anzac), 2nd (British), and 3rd (Anzac) Battalions of the Imperial Camel Corps, swinging in from the south-west, came under artillery fire from the German gunners behind El Magruntain. But camels can't be stampeded or even excited by shell fire. In fine precision the Cameliers swung away, dismounted, and in a huge segment of a circle advanced on the main Turkish redoubts. On their left the English and Scots Yeomanry dismounted, linked up, and pushed forward, their left resting on the sand-hills overlooking the Mediterranean. The New Zealanders, working wide, like a sheep-dog rounding up a big flock, executed a fine encircling movement, and, dismounting, attacked the position from the north-east. Abdul now found himself fighting for dear life, attacked from all sides, while a hail of shrapnel came from the British guns. The Krupp guns worked manfully, but soon a couple of them were put out of action. The German machine gunners, as at Romani and Maghdaba, handled their guns with great skill, but the rain of shells soon discounted their efficiency. On the other hand, the British machine guns swept up and down the Turkish trenches, and prevented .the garrison firing too freely at the attackers in the open. So with the Hong-Kong battery in support of the Camelry, and the Territorial gunners covering the advance of the Anzacs, the attack was pushed steadily on to the objective.

Aloft our airmen were busy, while the Taubes, splendidly handled, strove hard to prevent our aerial scouts from directing the fire of our artillery. There were thrilling air combats, but for the most part, those down below were too busy with their own affairs. Behind the lines the stretcher-bearers did wonderful work. Entirely indifferent to the bullets, which zipped into the sand all round, they rescued the wounded and carried them back to the safety of the ambulances.

The enemy air scouts kept their headquarters well informed as to the strength of the British attack. So with a view to preventing a repetition of the Maghdaba defeat, strong reinforcements were hurried up from Sheikh Neiran and Beersheba. These were the party held up by the New Zealanders. Had these reinforcements pushed on with vigour they might have changed the fortunes of the day. But the New Zealanders, as they approached, poured in a heavy fire from rifles and machine guns. So Abdul, probably overestimating the strength of the Maorilanders, gave over the attempt to relieve Rafa.

Meanwhile the accurate and well-sustained fire of our guns, maxims, and rifles at length achieved a superiority of fire over the garrison, which enabled the attackers to approach, by well-timed advances, nearer and nearer the Turkish trenches. The cordon tightened. An ever-closing circle menaced the defenders. When within striking distance, a glitter of steel flashed all round the circle. The British bayonets were getting ready for the final rush. Nearer and nearer they came, and then, with a final shout, charged straight at the enemy. Abdul stuck it until the gleaming bayonets were about 30 yards from his trenches, when discretion triumphed over valour, and up went the hands in surrender. By five o'clock the whole garrison had surrendered, and had been hurried back towards El Arish. About 300 enemy dead were buried, nearly 500 wounded men were cared for, and over 1600 unwounded prisoners were led away. They included 30 Turkish officers with their commander, the whole of the 603rd German Machine-gun Company, and some German officers, one of whom was caught riding in the town of Rafa. Our booty included 4 Krupp guns, 7 machine guns, 1600 rifles, 45,000 rounds of ammunition, 83 camels, and other warlike stores.

Our own casualties were heavier than at Maghdaba, but light considering the open ground over which they attacked. There were four officers and 68 men killed, and 31 officers and 384 men wounded. At this cost the last Turkish stronghold in Sinai was captured. The Sinai Campaign was over. The next phase of the war in the East would be in Turkish territory—in Palestine.

The Cameliers now jogged on back to El Arish for a well-earned spell. They missed several well-known faces round the fire at night. The officers grieved over the loss of Captain George Smith, Captain MacCullum, and Lieut. Linforth. But soldiers don't grieve long. It might be their turn next. Sergeant Blaine bolted down to Cairo for a holiday. All the way down he was thinking of a little angel in the 14th Australian General Hospital.

CHAPTER 11

The Ball—1

Sergeant Blaine, up in Cairo for a week's Christmas leave, made his first call at the Bints' Retreat. Flora was unfeignedly glad to see him. But he was far happier at seeing her.

"I've got a whole week's holiday, Fair Lady," he said, "and I hereby dedicate every minute to you."

Sister curtsied prettily in acknowledgement, then shaking her head, she said:

"It can't be done, sir."

"In the bright lexicon of youth," he said, "there is no such word as can't."

"In this old hospital," she retorted, "there seems to be nothing else. We can't go out or talk with anyone unless he be an officer. We can't dance. We can't stay out later than ten o'clock. Oh, Bob, if you could only see the list of 'thou shalt nots'! Then there is the Christmas Eve Dance at Shepheard's Hotel, and I can't go."

"Do you remember what the Irishman said to the Yankee guide at Niagara Falls? Well, the Yankee pointed down at the seething waters, and said grandiloquently that five million gallons of water rolled down there every second. The Irishman just looked over and said, 'Well! what's to hinder?'"

Sister laughed and said, "Oh, but there are several things to hinder me."

"Namely?"

"Well, Matron for one; and, anyhow, I'm in disgrace."

He whistled in mock seriousness.

"Oh, it's no joke," she persisted. "Some old cat told Matron that I had tea at Groppe's with some private soldiers. I said they were not private soldiers; they were 'Gentlemen of the Australian Light Horse.' But she couldn't see it. Then I went to Maadi to some awfully nice friends, and time simply flew, and I was an hour late in getting in. So I'm in the bad books, and no leave for a month."

"Then what's the good of my holiday?" he demanded.

"Oh, I'd risk anything to go to that ball." she cried, ignoring his query.

"Do you really mean that?"

"Yes," she said decisively. "I'm sick to death of this discipline. That proves I'm an Anzac. I want to discard this old uniform and wear pretty clothes and have a real good time again."

"Are you prepared to take the risk?"

"I just am," she asserted.

"Righto, we'll do it."

"We?"

"Why, of course," he replied. "I couldn't let you risk it on your own. Besides, I'll have to arrange for escort, introductions, and a host of things. Now, is Matron going?"

"Yes, with the P.M.O. and Sister Smith."

"Good; that simplifies matters. They can't come here and find you out."

"But she'll be there———"

"And will fail to recognise you," he added.

"Now, will you trust me to see the whole thing through?"

"Shake," she said.

****

The Principal Medical Officer's car drew up at the entrance to the Bints' Retreat. Matron and Sister Smith and the P.M.O. and Captain Evans entered, and just as they were moving off, Sister Livingstone hurried up with a big bouquet of flowers for Matron. "It's from the Australian Eleven, Matron, and they wish you a very happy Christmas."

"Oh, thank you, Sister Livingstone. I'm sorry you'll miss the ball."

"Maleesch," cried Sister, turning back to the hospital.

"I do wish you were coming," cried Captain Evans.

"Never mind. My turn next. Be sure to dance with my sister, and tell her I'll be in to see her tomorrow."

No sooner had the car moved off than Sister dashed into the Bints' Retreat. Sisters Douglas and Peters, sworn to secrecy, hurriedly dressed her in all her finery. Her fine silk dress that had remained so long at the bottom of her cabin trunk, her gorgeous ostrich feather fan, diamond-clasped osprey, and beautiful necklet, ear-rings, and bracelet, and brooch that her indulgent parent had given her—all were put on in record time. Both the Sisters kissed her and wished her luck.

"Oh, you look ravishing," cried Sister Peters, as she threw a big cloak over Flora and hurried out.

A beautiful closed-in motor-car, timing her exit to a second, glided up noiselessly. The door opened and she sprang in, and the car shot off like a Bristol fighter. A strong arm deftly surrounded her with rugs—for Cairo is very cold in midwinter.

"Oh, Bob," she cried, "I'm deliriously happy."

"You're going to be the belle of the ball tonight, Honey. All is going swimmingly. All that you have to remember is that you are Miss Mary Livingstone, sister of Flora; you arrived in Suez yesterday, came on to Cairo, and are leaving tomorrow to catch the boat again at Port Said. You are two years younger than Flora, and you are awfully sorry that she could not come to the ball. So that's that."

"And you?" she queried.

"Oh, I'm just Robert Smith, an Australian journalist. I've got a weak heart or cold feet. That's why I didn't enlist."

"It all seems plausible enough, but I wish we could have arrived before Matron."

"We will," he said, with a grin. "It was essential that she should see you back at the hospital as she left. That absolutely killed any suspicions she might have had. Then I closed the railway gates just as they came along, and the poor old Doc honked for five minutes before the old gatekeeper arrived."

"Yes," she replied, "that's great, but they are still five minutes ahead of us."

"Oh, but they are going to have an accident," he said prophetically. And as he spoke the lights flashed on a car stopped at the side of the Heliopolis Road, with the chauffeur sprawled beneath.

"Good for Jimmy!" cried Blaine as they flew past. "Now, as old Midgley used to say, 'We've got 'em stone cold.'"

"Bob," cried Flora, "I think you're wonderful. But suppose *we* had an accident?"

"Look behind," he said.

She looked through the window, and saw the light of another car a chain or so behind.

"Now I'm sure we'll win through."

Shepheard's Hotel, known to tourists all over the world, was a blaze of splendour. A brilliant throng crowded the hall, the piazza, and the corridors. The youth and beauty of Cairo were engaged in high revelry. The uniforms of the officers, though mostly khaki, added to the gaiety of the scene. Big Nubian waiters in baggy breeches and gold-laced coats hurried hither and yon, providing the necessary Eastern colouring to the picture. As Flora emerged from the cloak-room, Blaine, who had never before seen her except in her nurse's uniform, was entranced with her loveliness. The excitement of the venture had given an added colour to her cheeks and a brighter sparkle to her eyes. She moved with an easy grace that denoted perfect health and the joy of living. As she hesitated near the hall she found her way barred by a tall, bronzed gentleman in immaculate evening-dress.

"Bob!" she gasped. "I hardly knew you. You do look fine."

"There aren't enough beautiful adjectives in the English language," he said, "to describe how wonderful you are, Honey."

Then the orchestra gave forth the enticing strains of "Blue Danube," and they waltzed away to paradise.

"Oh, Flora," he whispered passionately, "you're the most beautiful thing God ever made."

"Please, Bob," she pleaded, "I'm so happy; but don't give me any more to think of tonight. It might spoil everything. But you do dance divinely."

He vouchsafed only the gentlest pressure of her hand in acknowledgement of the compliment. He had a curious fear that he might suddenly clasp her in his, arms before the whole crowd. All dancers have experienced the psychology of the ballroom. There is always a belle of the ball. One girl or one couple in an incredibly short time become the cynosure of all eyes. It may be a certain skill in the execution of the newfangled Tango or an audacious display of silken hose that catches the eye. Sometimes, as in this case, it is sheer physical beauty. Flora and Bob had hardly thrice circled the room before they instinctively felt that nearly everyone was looking at them. They were certainly the handsomest couple there, if not exactly the best dancers. A perfect waltzer, Blaine had never found time to master the intricacies of the later-day dances. Sister was the best dancer on the Hunter River. So in the gay throng these two danced, deliriously happy—Blaine, however, frowning as he realised the unexpected social success his partner had instantly made. He had foreseen and provided for every contingency save this.

As the music ceased, many eyes followed them towards the gardens. Blaine realised that no one in the crowd knew them, and every girl in the hall was demanding, "Who is she?" which was not exactly what he desired So he kept his eyes working overtime till he sighted his good friends of Maadi. He took Flora across the lawn, and presenting her to Mr. and Mrs. Hart, said:

"Permit me to present Miss Mary Livingstone of Sydney. She has just landed in Cairo, and goes on, *via* Port Said, to London tomorrow."

To Mrs. Hart he said:

"Your duty as chaperon is no sinecure, for the whole army in Egypt will be besieging you soon."

CHAPTER 12

The Ball—2

Blaine had taken the precaution to shave his moustache and wear pince-nez, so in his dress-suit he was pretty confident that none of the Light Horse or Camel Corps officers would recognise him. He hurried through the hall and out into Sharia Kamel just in time to see the P.M.O.'s party drive up. After they had entered the hotel he went across to the chauffeur and pressed a note into his hand.

"Jimmy, old sport," he cried, "you're a brick."

Jimmy Eagleton stared for a second, blew a long but subdued whistle, and then exclaimed:

"Well, I'm blowed! If you just don't beat the band, Blainey. O'course you won't get court-martialled at all."

"I'll risk that, Jimmy. Now what time is the car ordered for?" "Eleven-thirty."

"Good! Now do you think you could arrange for your lights to peter out on the way home?"

"It'll cost another hundred disasters baksheesh," said Jimmy.

"Righto," agreed Blaine. "You see, Sister must be here and Matron must see her here when Matron leaves. Yet we've got to be back at least a quarter of an hour ahead. I've got Pat to halt you and take your name near the old barracks. That will give us five minutes. Then, if all goes well—tomorrow night at the National."

Hurrying in, Blaine found Flora the centre of a gallant

throng of Australian and New Zealand and British officers. Even though he had previously booked three waltzes and two two-steps, he could not resist a pang of jealousy as the officers clamoured for the honour.

Mrs. Hart was keenly enjoying the situation, being tremendously proud of her protégée. Flora was in the seventh heaven. She had just danced with General Cox, and gallant old 'Fighting Charlie' had paid her some very pretty compliments, then brought all the Light Horse officers along.

As the music suddenly burst into the lively strains of the "Frog Puddles Two-Step," Blaine with difficulty insinuated his way to the front and bore her off in triumph. They were entering the ballroom when they encountered General Cox and the Matron's party. Blaine gently pressed her hand as it rested on his arm, and whispered, "Bluff hard, Honey." The introductions followed.

"Oh, Matron, I am pleased to meet you," said Flora. "My sister has often written nice things of you. I'm so sorry she could not come tonight, but you will let her come in tomorrow to see me, won't you?"

Matron was surprised into an assent, when the P.M.O. remarked:

"You are startlingly like your sister, Miss Livingstone."

"May we see you after this dance?" interrupted Blaine. "I hate to lose a second of this music." And they whirled away with joyous abandon.

"Beautifully done. You've got Matron thinking hard, and poor Sister Smith is gasping."

As the hospital quartet gazed after the pair, Matron remarked:

"The resemblance is wonderful, but I think this girl is a little bit taller and slighter than her sister."

"And much prettier," interpolated Sister Smith.

Captain Evans smiled enigmatically, and then vouchsafed:

"No two sisters were ever so extraordinarily alike."

Heedless of the comment, Blaine and Flora threaded their way amongst the dancers as happy as a pair of school children on holiday. He had passed the forbidden notice-board which said, "Out of Bounds for N.C.O.'s and Men," and for a brief while again he tasted the joys of the life he had known. Pretty Cairenes, who had condescendingly given him a cup of tea in a canteen some months before, now smiled frankly on him and said he danced beautifully. Field officers and generals, whom he had punctiliously saluted that morning, were now inviting him to partake of iced coffee cocktails. He grinned sardonically at the farce of it all. As an Australian soldier, an original Nineteen-fourteener, wounded on Gallipoli and at Romani, he dared not enter these hallowed precincts. But as an alleged slacker, a mere civilian, he came unchallenged. And Flora, curiously enough, voiced the sentiments he only thought.

"Isn't it curious," she said. "As a nurse, doing my little bit for Old England, I'm forbidden to dance, and I must go home early. But as a civvie slacker, I can dance the red stars to their death."

As the music ceased with a snap, not dying away like a waltz, but suddenly, with exaggerated syncopation, the dancers all crowded, laughing and chatting gaily, into the vestibule and thence to the gardens. The trees and palms were all hung with coloured lights and Chinese lanterns. The fountain splashed musically. The lawn and paths were dotted with dancers, two and two, revelling in the cold night air after the heated dance hall. Now and then Blaine and Flora, in darkened corners, stumbled across couples very close together. Still, it was Christmas time, and kissing goes by favour; and Cairo is the world's playground.

"I wonder who is my next partner," suddenly exclaimed Flora, as the seductive strains of the "Barcarolle" percolated through the doors and out into the still night air. Halting under a lamp she glanced at her programme. "Brown. Now who is Brown?"

"That's my pagan name," Blaine admitted guiltily. "You see, I couldn't sprawl Smith all over your programme, could I?"

"Young man," she admonished, "you're incorrigible. If you don't get on in this world, it won't be for want of push. Still, I'm so deliriously happy tonight, I can't refuse you anything; and anyway I'd hate to waste the 'Barcarolle' on a stranger. It's a gorgeous waltz."

Blaine always remembered that waltz as the most perfect soul-satisfying dance in all his life. "Flora," he cried, as they swung to the very poetry of motion, "you're perfect. I've never till this minute prayed for a night that's a thousand years long. If I'm court-martialled and shot at dawn tomorrow, it's been well worth it. Tonight's the night."

And Flora's heart was beating so joyously that she dared not voice her reply.

At the door going out they encountered Matron again and Sister Smith.

"We are having a little midnight supper," said Bob; "I do hope your quartet will join us."

"Thanks so much, Mr. Smith," replied Matron, "but we have to be back at the hospital before twelve."

"Oh, here's the Colonel," cried Flora. "Surely he can give himself permission to remain out late on Christmas Eve."

"I'm sorry it cannot be done," said the P.M.O., smiling.

Flora just then was claimed by a gallant Camelier and whisked off for a fox-trot. And as Blaine watched her perfect grace and radiant beauty he found himself building beautiful castles in the air. . . .

"Bob, you're in love."

He turned and encountered Mr. Hart smiling at his side. Curiously enough he never troubled to deny the soft impeachment. He only ejaculated, "My God, isn't she just perfect!"

"Here, you want a drink," asserted the matter-of-fact friend. "Come on."

On the way to the bar he chuckled and said, "It's the best

joke Cairo has seen since the Anzacs scandalised the good folk by putting a nose-bag on the charger of Soliman Pasha's statue. Mrs. Hart has received a dozen pressing invitations for Flora, and hundreds of inquiries about her. And she's come to the end of her tether. She's told wonderful tales of how Flora fought bushrangers and escaped from wild natives and rode buckjumpers. Oh, the Gyppie *Mail* will be quite readable tomorrow."

The four of them, Mr. and Mrs. Hart, Flora and Bob, were out on the piazza, where a dainty little supper had been laid Filling his glass Mr. Hart raised it aloft and gave the toast:

"To the belle of the ball."

Shortly afterwards the P.M.O., the Matron, Captain Evans, and Sister Smith emerged. Flora hastened to bid them goodnight, while Bob signalled to the waiter for his car. The party had scarcely moved off in the hospital car before the four conspirators had hurried forth into Bob's automobile. He and Mr. Hart sat in front, while in the roomy, enclosed tonneau, Flora and Mrs. Hart got busy.

"You've got about a quarter of an hour to change," Blaine told Flora as the car glided after the P.M.O.'s machine.

"Well," exclaimed Matron as they moved off, "I could never have believed such a resemblance possible."

"It certainly is unique," concurred the P.M.O.

Captain Evans in his seat in front smiled grimly. As the car swung round the broad way and approached the railway station, a native policeman halted them and drew attention to their dim lights. Jimmy jumped out and took a shocking time fixing them up. Suddenly Captain Evans laughed.

"Say, Colonel, did you ever read *Dr. Jekyll and Mr. Hyde?*"

"Yes; why?"

"Oh, nothing," replied Evans. "I was just thinking."

Shortly after midnight Matron and Sister Smith entered the ward where was housed the Australian Eleven. They found Sister Livingstone seated at the little table writing in the ward-book.

"How are all your patients, Sister?" asked Matron.

"Oh, they are all doing nicely," replied Flora in the bored tones of the night-duty nurse. "I hope you enjoyed the ball. Did you meet my little sister? Isn't she pretty?"

Chapter 13

The Sister

Amongst the Egyptian words destined to be incorporated in the Australian language, the most popular are 'baksheesh' and 'maleesch.' Neither of these has an exact equivalent in our own tongue. Even as ' baksheesh ' is the first word that the Gyppie baby learns to lisp, so was it the first word to fall on the ears of the Australians in Egypt. No child in the land of the Pharaohs is too young to accost strangers with the plea for baksheesh, and no decrepit old derelict too old to do the same. Blessed word—like unto Mesopotamia—it is with the Egyptian from the cradle to the grave; it permeates everywhere; it puts the finishing touch on every commercial transaction, no matter how trifling or how great.

And maleesch is more blessed still. It expresses, oh, so wonderfully, the spineless, emasculated spirit of resignation which is the foundation of the fellahin's philosophy. A subject race, prey to all the warlike nations of the earth for centuries, exclaims at each change of masters, 'Maleesch'. The plagues of Egypt come and go, and the fellah, with imperturbable stoicism, says, 'Maleesch'. He is knocked down by a motorcar, 'Maleesch'. He dies, and the neighbouring fellahin cry, 'Maleesch'. And the word cannot be translated into English. The nearest approach is, 'What matter.' So in days to come Australian settlers, viewing the devastation brought by fires and floods and drought, will grin and exclaim, 'Maleesch'. There are other words curious and expressive adorning the Anzac's vocabulary, but the only other necessary to mention here is 'bint'. A bint is, in short, a girl. So we will not be surprised if some day an Australian on London Bridge greets a countrywoman with the cheery ejaculation, 'Saieeda, Bint'.

Which brings us to the fact that the nurses' quarters of the hospital were always known as the 'Bints' Retreat'. Things had been very lively out East of Suez, and the hospital trains had been working overtime. And back in the hospitals of Cairo were thousands of soldiers wounded and maimed and stricken and blinded. Here was all the hideous aftermath of battle.

Sister Livingstone had been toiling with only the briefest respite for several days, and was now in her little cubicle in the 'Bints' Retreat' resting. She had been too tired to accept kind invitations of Captain Evans and others to dinner at Shepheard's. The Doctor had been very assiduous in his attentions to Sister for a long time now, but his suit had made but little headway. When the nurses in friendly raillery—maybe rivalry—chided Flora about the Doctor, she laughingly replied that she loved every single soldier in the A.I.F. If she had a preference she hardly knew it herself, though every week she received a cheery letter from a big sergeant in the Cameliers, and once a month she wrote a gracious letter in reply.

Lately she had also received from him the first few copies of the Cameliers' Journal *Barrak*, a quaint little paper edited somewhere in Wadi Ghuzzie, and written by men of the I.C.C. all over Egypt and Sinai and Southern Palestine. Sergeant Blaine had interpolated explanatory paragraphs throughout the pages wherever there was a reference he thought Sister might not understand. So she turned the leaves idly, smiling proudly at the devil-may-care spirit of the soldiers, which made them make light of all their hardships and see only the cheerful side of everything. The heterogeneous nature of the I.C.C. was well shown by a skit by Corporal 'Cuss' called 'Abbassia'.

From the farthest isles of Orkney,
From the edge of the Sudan,
From the flats of Murrumbidgee,
Or the purlieus of Japan,
From amid the waving pampas,
Or the banks of Windermere,
They have gathered, gathered, gathered
To the huts of Abbassia.

He whose single thought was salmon
Met the rogue who poached for pearls,
And the Billjim made a cobber
Of the darling of the girls:
The guardsman and the terrier,
The plutocrat and peer—
All are jumbled up together
In the huts of Abbassia.

If you seek for information
On polo, maps, or gin,
Beer, beauty, or ballistics,
You can find it all within:
If you seek the heat of battle,
Or you're finding life too drear—
Go and join 'The Curse of Egypt'
In the huts of Abbassia.

The Light Horseman considers himself a cut above the infantryman and several cuts above the Camelier. Of course neither the infantryman nor the Camelier endorses this view, though the Light Horsemen who have joined the I.C.C., when they do get up to Cairo for a holiday, like to put on their old leggings and spurs just for old times' sake. Hence "The Cameliers' Lament."

When we lob in from the desert with a thirst that's worth a crown,
Heavy laden with piastres, and the mood to paint the town,
Having left our smellful camels somewhere east of El Arish,
Then the world is full of sunshine, and we've just one little wish—
For feathers and leggings and spurs,
Feathers and leggings and spurs.

On the desert we're 'Camels'; we're rough, rude, and coarse men,
But when up on leave we're once more 'Light Horsemen',
With feathers and leggings and spurs.

We mooch up to the Kit Store, Abbassia, like a thief,
Like a sneaking, crawling Gyppi who has pinched some bully beef:
Shorts and puttees are discarded and we don our breeks again,
We fling away our jamboks and we swish a little cane.
Oh, feathers and leggings and spurs,
Feathers and leggings and spurs.

Out East with the 'Hooshters' we're rough, rude, and coarse men,
But round about Cairo we're 'Pukka Light Horsemen',
With feathers and leggings and spurs.

Our boots are brightly polished, like the old-time Kiwi Lancers,
We join the gentle soirée and we mingle with the dancers,
Till a maiden, gently 'sniffing', knocks us all into a lump,
By disdainfully exclaiming, "Camels do give me the hump",
Tho' plumed and booted and spurred,
Plumed and booted and spurred.

Once you join Camels you're smellful and coarse men:
Goodbye to the swank of the Kiwi Light Horsemen,
All plumed and booted and spurred.

The lines by Captain Morgan, however, seemed to sum up finely the unique qualities of the I.C.C.:

I.C.C.
Known from the 'beer' in Shepheard's Bar
To the 'U' in unsurveyed;

Silent under a watching star
Or by our dust betrayed.
Where Kharga blossoms 'mid western rock,
Or Sollum fronts on the shore,
By river bank or 'mid grazing flock,
The Imperial Camel Corps.
When the mounted troops on Rafa dash,
Or lost in the drifting sand;
Where successive waves of battle clash,
Or the lonely outposts stand;
Any and every job we know,
Used as a transport corps.
Shelled and bombed by friend and foe,
The Ikonas of the war.

Chapter 14

The Soldier

There were three battles round about Gaza. The first and second were costly defeats, involving a loss to the Egyptian Expeditionary Force of at least twelve thousand men in killed and wounded. The enemy losses are variously estimated, but from the nature of the conflict they must have been less than ours.

So the victorious Desert Column after its uninterrupted series of successes from Romani to Rafa was at last brought to a standstill, and the German General commanding the Turkish forces was able to send this delightful message to the British Commander: "I have defeated you in the field, but you have beaten me in the communiqué."

The enemy had taken up a strong defensive position with Gaza as its culminating point, the right flank resting on the Mediterranean and the left on Beersheba. General Murray made his dispositions with a view to (1) preventing the threatened withdrawal of the Turks from the Beersheba side, (2) capturing the Wadi Ghuzzie so as to protect the advance of the railway from Rafa, and (3) seizing Gaza by a *coup de main* and cutting off the garrison. It was in this third and vital objective the British failed.

As usual, the Anzac Mounted Division opened the ball, swinging east and north and heading for Beit Durdis. In their wake came the Imperial Mounted Division and the Imperial Camel Corps. Crossing the Wadi Ghuzzie the Cavalry and Camelry pushed on round the left wing of the Turkish army. The rapid move of the Light Horse took the enemy by surprise, and a squadron of the 7th Light Horse captured the commander of one of the Turkish Divisions. The dumbfounded general heard a wild Colonial yell, his carriage was surrounded, and a stentorian voice cried,

"Here, give us your———sword."

Great enterprises hang on little incidents. A fall of rain or a passing mist may decide the fate of a nation. It is the opinion of several British generals that had there been, no mist on the morning of 26th March the first battle of Gaza would have been won. Be that as it may, the whole plan of our operations was very seriously retarded by a heavy mist which enveloped the whole countryside. Spreading like a pall over the battlefield before dawn, it did not clear off till eight o'clock.

While General Chetwode's Desert Column was mopping up the country north-east of Gaza the infantry moved forward from the south. The 53rd Division (Major-General Dallas) pushed in, and after dogged fighting captured the Ali Muntar Ridge. The 54th Division held Sheikh Abbas, while for some reason or other the 52nd Division was kept back in reserve. In the late afternoon the situation was full of possibilities of victory, though the cavalry and camelry on the right were strenuously withstanding the onslaught of a continuous stream of Turkish reinforcements. However, during the night the Anzacs were withdrawn; the 53rd Division being thus 'in the air' were compelled to retire, likewise the 54th Division, and by daylight the army—beaten when victory was just within its grasp—had fallen back to the west of the Wadi Ghuzzie. It is estimated that the Turks lost 8000 and the British 4000. The enemy communiqué gives different figures entirely. But our captures were about 950 Turks and Germans, with two Austrian guns gallantly captured and held by the New Zealanders.

Preparations were immediately made for a second attack. But the enemy had been reinforced till there were five divisions of infantry, one of cavalry, and a full complement of artillery ready to dispute the possession of Gaza. The hills were lined with trenches and redoubts. Machine guns dotted the entire front. In view of the fact that the Turks had constructed trenches and wire entanglements on the fine south, and east towards Beersheba, Sir Archibald Murray presumed that any encircling movement by the mounted divisions was out of the question. In this conviction his strategy differed from that subsequently and successfully pursued by General Allenby.

The second battle of Gaza therefore began on 17th April by the capture of the Sheikh Abbas-Mansura Ridge to the south and south-east of Gaza. Tanks were thrown into the fight, but as there was no element of surprise in their projection they were not an unqualified success. Three of them lumbering along in full view of the enemy artillery were pounded with shells and put out of action. However, the first objective, the Sheikh Abbas-Mansura Ridge, was captured without many casualties. Then came two days' further preparation and the final assault. The guns of two British monitors and the French battleship *Requin* made excellent practice on the Gaza defences and also got busy amongst the Turks assembling for counter-attacks. Three British infantry divisions—one Welsh, one Scots, and one English—were launched in the main attack. The 53rd Division, in the face of a tremendous fusillade from rifles and machine guns, charged and captured Samson's Ridge and Delilah's Neck on the south side of the town. The 52nd and 54th Divisions were given the herculean task of securing the Ali Muntar Ridge and redoubts and the Khirbet Sihan line of trenches, east of the town; while Sheikh Abbas and the redoubts farther east were the objective of the Cameliers.

Abdul had not wasted the respite given him since 26th March. In twenty-four days the German engineers had transformed the hillside into a citadel. With great gallantry the 54th and 52nd and Anzac Cameliers charged the formidable line of trenches. This was the signal for the enemy artillery, which opened a terrific bombardment of the attacking line. They searched the whole area with wonderful precision. Shrapnel seemed to tear up every inch of the ground. Though facing a veritable avalanche of shells without a vestige of cover, the long khaki line never wavered. But the path they had trod was dotted with still, crumpled-up figures. Then as the line neared the hill it seemed as if hell were let loose among them. Mingling with the roar of the artillery now came the incessant rattle of dozens of Maxims. The charging line melted away like wheat before the scythe. Successive waves pushed on, but Outpost Hill was a hornet's nest of machine guns. This redoubt effectually held up the 52nd and incidentally exposed the 54th to a devastating enfilade fire from the east.

But two companies of Anzac Camelry on the right would not be denied. Leaving a trail of casualties behind, they charged right into the Turkish redoubt and bayoneted the few Turks who had not fled. But the infantry on their left could not advance. The right was 'in the air'. They were immediately shelled by the enemy batteries and a counter-attack followed. But the heroic remnant with well-directed rifle fire held off their assailants. One spot of the main objective had been gained. But without reinforcements it could never be held. From flank and front came the enemy rifle and machine-gun fire. Then, that their cup of joy might be filled to overflowing, they became a target for their own gunners. Five messengers were sent back to say that the redoubt had been captured, but not one got through. Finally, when their ammunition had been exhausted and every officer killed and wounded except Lieut. Archie Campbell, and 75 per cent, of their number casualties, the Cameliers decided to make a getaway. About thirty unwounded men returned to the battalion.

Meantime about a dozen of their comrades in the next redoubt were less fortunate. They had fired their last cartridge when a Turkish counter-attack ten times their strength swarmed over, and after a fierce bayonet *mêlée* took the remnant prisoners. As they were being lined up and marched off, two troopers of No. 3 Company, Kelly and Storey, decided that Stamboul was no good to them.

"How about it, Bert?"

"Righto, Kelly. Let her go."

Then, before their captors could guess their intention, the pair leaped the parapet and ran like startled hares towards the Wadi Ghuzzie. The Turkish line suddenly began to spit fire all along. Machine guns took up the chase. Bullets zipped all around the adventurous pair, but by some freak of good fortune neither was hit. Amid the wild cheers of their comrades they fell exhausted into the wadi, Kelly boasting bullet holes through his hat.

It now became a matter of throwing in the reserves—74th Division—and risking all on a further assault, or digging in. Already there had been about 8000 casualties. The G.O.C. Eastern Force and the Divisional Commanders advised against a resumption. So the army dug in, and the second battle of Gaza had been fought and lost.

Chapter 15

The Soldier

Way back in the centre of Sinai, where the mountains rise gaunt and rugged from the shining sands, where gazelle and ibex roam almost unmolested by the hunter, where the summer sun scorches like a furnace and the winter rains lie frozen in the rock holes at dawn; here, where the Bedouin is monarch of all he surveys, went the Pilgrim Patrol.

Small scouting patrols, starting out from Ayun Mousa for a few days' scouring of the hills, had not been entirely immune from attack. Several had been sniped from the ranges. An English officer and some Yeomanry had been killed. The Bedouin will not fight, but he does practise the ambuscade. So the Pilgrim Patrol was fairly strong, 50 Anzac Cameliers, with a couple of machine-guns; enough to account for several hundred Bedouins should they prove troublesome—which they did not; enough to mop up any Turkish patrols that might be encountered—which they were not.

Now in the centre of the Sinai Peninsula, hidden away in the wadis, leading the same nomadic life that they did thousands of years ago, live several thousands of Bedouin Arabs. These are divided into the three inevitable groups—sympathetic, apathetic, antipathetic—and the greatest of these is antipathetic. Most of the men of the tribe follow their sheikh, who may be influenced by fear or gold, as the case may be. Some are loyally pro-British; others having heard the musical clink of German gold have sided with the Turks. The remainder, following the spineless example of Mr. Facing-both-ways, sit at ease and watch the way the cat jumps.

Thus it transpired that in the early days of the war, when the Turks overran Sinai, even to the bounds of the Red Sea, the bulk of the Bedouins saw the Crescent in the ascendant. Abu Zenima was captured. Tor was invested. El Arish and Nekhl were in the hands of the enemy. Hundreds of Turkish rifles, with abundant ammunition, were distributed amongst the Bedouins. It took many weary months and many hot fights finally to drive the invader back into Palestine. But in the fastnesses of the mountains the Bedouins remained, and, of course, the Turkish rifles remained with them. But the fiery Crescent waned. Cameliers and Light Horse patrols scoured the desert sands and the wadis and the oases till the Bedouin saw the game was up Most of them swore allegiance, and handed in their rifles. Many hid their rifles underground, and with protestations of loyalty greeted the Anzacs who invaded their villages. Smoke signals gave warning more readily than the telegraph. And away in the centre of Southern Sinai were still hundreds of Bedouins with Turkish rifles ready to snipe at a few adventurous scouts, or fawn with Uriah-Heep humility on a strong patrol. Hence the three weeks' stunt of the Pilgrim Patrol.

Australians are now aware that the Camel Corps can exist for days at a time on the desert without the aid of wells or the A.S.C. In winter it is no hardship for the camels to go for over a week without a drink, especially if there is any herbage about. So the three weeks' trek of the Pilgrim Patrol necessitated merely the prearrangement of depots at two particular points for replenishing the tucker bags, grain sacks, and water fantasses, which done, the party, following in Moses' footsteps, went forth into the wilderness.

It does not serve any purpose here to detail the number of Bedouin villages visited and rifles confiscated, nor record the tribes which came into Abu Zenima and Tor to swear allegiance. Rather is it the intention to describe the visit to far-famed Jebel Mousa, or Mount Sinai, where back at the dawn of history Moses gave to the Children of Israel those Ten Commandments which have become the code of ethics for the civilised world. It was because of the pilgrimage to Jebel Mousa, and the visit to the famous old convent of St. Katharine, that this particular patrol won the sobriquet of the Pilgrim Patrol.

There is some difference of opinion amongst learned archaeologists as to which is the actual mountain where Moses received the Law. Four peaks in Sinai are mentioned, and each has some claim to consideration. But the general consensus of erudite opinion leads to the belief that either Jebel Serbal or Jebel Mousa is the actual spot. The Pilgrim Patrol—making no claim whatever to erudition—endorses without prejudice the claims of Jebel Mousa (Mount of Moses) for three potent reasons:

1. The ancient Greek Church, convinced that Jebel Mousa was where Moses received the Law, here 1600 years ago established the famous monastery.

2. Round Jebel Mousa are wells and wadis and several thousand acres of green pasture-land, admirably adapted for the camping-ground of the Children of Israel.

3. The vicinity of Jebel Serbal is rocky and barren, with no possible place for the Israelites to have camped to receive the Law.

The road to Jebel Mousa, through the wadis and over the hills, is so exceedingly rough and rugged that one marvels how camels in full marching order could possibly have negotiated it. There is a very narrow opening, just like a crack in the face of the mountains, and it is here that the Wadi Isleh escapes from the gargantuan grip of the hills and debouches on to the Plain of Oda. Into this picturesque defile, with mountains towering up thousands of feet on either side like frowning bastions, went the patrol. How many centuries of rain and wind and flood had it taken to carve that passage through the granite rocks?

It was the season of the winter rains. A couple of thunderstorms had drenched the Cameliers. Here and there the resultant slime on the bed of the wadi had produced such a precarious foothold that the camels at times slithered and slipped like novices on skates, flopping in the mud, throwing their riders into the mire, to the huge delight of all except the actual performers. The Wadi Isleh here and there opened out to the width of a decent river. Anon it closed in to a narrow gorge of barely sufficient space to allow the passage of the camels. Here it was smooth as the sands of Manly Beach. Anon the path was strewn with rocks and boulders, forbidding enough to bar progress until an improvised road had been constructed. In places the limpid waters, rippling lazily along the bed of the wadi, would suddenly disappear into the receptive sand. Farther along it would bubble up merrily like a spring, and continue its interrupted course towards the sea. Here and there were clumps of date palms, or stunted trees or wells, or Bedouin encampments. Charcoal-burning is the Bedouins' only industry, and many were encountered with their patient camels or donkeys heavily laden with charcoal, making for Tor, whence it is shipped to Suez.

Leaving the comparatively good going of the wadi bed, the ill-defined track led over rough, boulder-strewn plateaus down into other wadis, over more hills, down mountain paths offering a most precarious foothold, till in the fullness of time the patrol camped under the lee of the famous Jebel Mousa. Here was the quaint old monastery founded, so tradition hath it, by Constantine the Great in the early part of the fourth century, and completed by Justinian later on. Considering its sacred associations, and its rich literary and artistic treasures, this is surely one of the most interesting spots on the face of the earth. Incidentally it may be mentioned that although the records go back for hundreds of years, there is no record of any Australians having visited there, so the Pilgrim Patrol has the unique distinction of being the first Australians to set foot on Mount Sinai.

The adherents of the Monastery of St. Katharine are mostly Russians and Greeks, and Father Polycarpus and the priests under his authority graciously showed us through the old chapel, with its wonderful old paintings, quaint mosaics, gorgeous vestments, its gems and jewels, sacred relics, ancient effigies, and priceless works of art. The library contains some of the oldest Greek, Arabic, and Syrian Bibles and manuscripts, and it is available for inspection by scholars and scientists; but the distance from civilisation renders the cost of the pilgrimage almost prohibitive. The beautiful effigy of St. Katharine merits a special notice. The lower part of the body is encased in a dress of solid silver. The bodice is beaten gold. The face is of coloured enamel, while on the head is a crown of gold blazing with precious stones. In a specially-made, richly-chased casket is kept the mummified head of St. Katharine wearing a golden tiara inset with gems.

In an anteroom adjoining the altar is the reputed spot where Moses saw the burning bush. The Biblical story was vividly brought to mind by old Father Polycarpus saying, "Take your boots from off your feet, for you stand on holy ground." A beaten brass table, wonderfully decorated, marks the spot. In the little chamber are many old paintings of scenes recorded in Genesis and Exodus, some beautiful mosaics and inlaid mother-of-pearl work. And near by, growing vigorously by the chapel wall, was a bush not unlike a brier, which we were assured was a lineal descendant of the actual burning bush of Moses.

There is a charnel-house adjoining the convent, and here, stacked in a gruesome pile, are the skeletons of the priests who throughout the centuries lived and died at Mount Sinai. On a chair at the door was the uncanny spectacle of old Stephanus the doorkeeper, propped up in the attitude in which he was killed many years ago. In a corner were several other skeletons, and on inquiry we were graciously informed that these were the remains of *visitors* who had died there.

As the Cameliers saddled up and once more trekked out into the wilderness, followed by the benediction of old Father Polycarpus, the convent bells pealed out a joyous message. But some of our irrepressibles reckoned it was because they were so mighty glad the rough unshaven Anzacs had departed in peace.

When we first saw the Mount it was shrouded in a snow-white mantle of cloud, even as it was when Moses of old ascended to receive the Ten Commandments. The height of Jebel Mousa is about 6000 ft. above sea-level, and when the patrol bivouacked there it was so bitterly cold that the water in our canvas water-bags froze solid, while a sheet of ice had to be broken through before the men could dip at the convent well. After an all too brief sojourn at this absorbingly interesting spot the patrol made across the flat where it is almost certain the Israelites camped, and trekked northward over more hills, along the sandy beds of more wadis, past many other spots of Biblical interest, till, still following in the footsteps of the Israelites, they crossed the border at Rafa and camped once more in Palestine.

Chapter 16

The Sister

In the silence of the night Sister sat writing. The ward was in semi-darkness Save for her little table where a shaded globe directed the light on her paper. She wrote:

> I have just been making the acquaintance of the Cameliers, Daddy. They have guest nights up at the officers' mess every week, and it's great fun. And they are a fine devil-may-care lot of officers. Quite a lot are old Original Nineteen-fourteeners, and what exciting adventures and hairbreadth escapes they could tell—if they only would. But they won't talk—at least about themselves. Some of them, with set lines round their eyes and a sprinkling of grey hairs on young heads, bear mute testimony to the nerve-wrecking Gallipoli days. Others are later arrivals from Australia. Quite a lot of them have risen from the ranks. In the old days 'risen from the ranks' had a distinctive significance, as you know, but amongst the rank and file of our 1st Division were hundreds of men of good old Australian families, whose education and professional or business standing were much better than many who, instead of enlisting at the outset, hung back for the Officers' Training Schools.
>
> As a matter of fact,—here's a confession, Daddy

dear,—the Camelier I am most interested in is only a sergeant. And the curious thing is that his section officer is a man from the same office, much junior to my Camelier, and in every way his inferior. But that is the fortune of war.

Oh, Daddy, I've met the general. He's awfully nice, and he looks too young to be a general. He surely has command of the most interesting and truly Imperial force in the whole army. For in the Imperial Camel Corps are Australians, New Zealanders, Indians, and South Africans, besides men from every part of the old country. More than half the whole I.C.C. are Australians, and of the original companies all were Gallipoli men. I sat next to the general at mess. He's got a breast-full of medals. He comes from the Duke of Cornwall's Light Infantry, and is still under forty years of age. His military career began in the South African War and continued through the Somali Campaign of 1903-4, where he won the V.C., and the Soudan Campaign of 1910. He joined the Egyptian army in 1905, and won his Military Cross in the Soudan in 1914. In January 1916 he went to Abbassia to raise and command four companies of Camelry. But the I.C.C. has grown and grown to its present dimensions.

There were several other distinguished Cameliers present at the last Guest Night, for the Camel Brigade was spelling at Rafa.

I met Colonel Langley, a Melbournian, who is about the only colonel I know who plays rugby with his battalion team. He also possesses a voice. Colonel De Lancy Forth, also a Victorian, has seen quite a lot of service and looks a typical British cavalry officer. Perhaps the most popular of all the senior officers is Colonel Mills, from sunny New South Wales. His men swear by him, and he in turn has a wonderful faith in, and appreciation of, the Australian Camelier. 'They'll do me' is a favourite expression of his, summing up his confidence in the boys.

Some English officers also were gathered round the festive board. Everyone in the Camel Corps knows Captain Barber. He holds autocratic sway amongst the details at Abbassia and fills all newcomers with feelings of dread. But his bark is far worse than his bite. A little while back Captain Barber was presented with the Order of the Nile decoration, which event prompted Captain Morgan to perpetuate the following effusion:

Captain Jas. Barber, O.N.
There was joy among the waiters, there was joy in Shepheard's Bar,
And the gloomy cocktail-mixer just contrived to raise a smile,
For the crowd kept growing deeper till it stretched both near and far,
When Barber got the Order of the Nile.
His regiment never knew him, but there's plenty more who do,
In the Horse and Guns and Camelry and Foot,
And they were very lucky who could see the evening through
And not receive the Order of the Boot.
There's rumour that he's getting yet a decoration higher
To recompense his service to the State.
He's merited the Ribbon of the Star of Stana Schwaya
For his lifelike imitation—Harry Tate.
There are various decorations: there's the Order of the Bath,
Very comforting when evening shadows lag;
And that frequent hard-earned honour—which is often
   for the Staff—
The Ethiopian Gold-Embroidered Bag.
I've seen 'em all distributed—and sometimes seen 'em earned;
But I shan't forget for quite a goodish while
That evening—or the morning when my head there-after burned—
When Barber got the Order of the Nile.

Major Buxton, Earl Winterton, Captain Tredennick, and Lieutenant Newson represented the English companies, while there was a host of Australian officers whose names I'll never remember. I know there were four Lieutenant Matthews, and they were differentiated as Camel Matt, Irish Matt, English Matt, and Sailor Matt. Then there were 'Fairy' and 'Togo' and 'Sporto' and 'Chum' and 'Cash' and 'Goldie' and 'Gulliver' and 'Buck' and 'Sandy' and 'Doc' and 'Nick' and 'Dusty' and 'Dickie' and 'Kess' and 'J. P.' and 'Robo' and 'Heppie', and, as the social scribes say, 'others too numerous to mention'. There were singing and elocutionary efforts, and the gramophone filled in the gaps. Of course, Heppie recited. It was positively his last public appearance in Abbassia, for the next day he was out on the desert trying his camel's paces, when an aeroplane swooped down and knocked him flying, while his startled camel started for the skyline. Heppie is now down in the officers' ward with a broken arm and other injuries, but he's as full of heart as a lion.

Oh, Daddy, do you know Colonel Todd? He's one of the livest officers in the whole of the A.I.F., and a real genial soul. He commands the 10th Light Horse Regiment, which has seen probably more fighting than any unit in the whole E.E.F. Well, he was there, and so was Colonel J. M. Arnott, who at Moascar has done wonderful work for the A.I.F. Mrs. Arnott also was there. She has been doing a lot of generous self-sacrificing work for the Red Cross here in Cairo., With her were Mrs. Featherstonhaugh, Mrs. Davies, and Miss Rentoul. The Anzacs in Egypt owe a deep debt of gratitude to these four ladies for all they have done to lighten the soldier's burden. Every sick and wounded Light Horseman or Camelier landing in at the hospital is met by one of these ladies and given a bag of comforts from home.

Does it interest you, Daddy, this idle chatting about

the folk I meet over here? Or would you prefer that I should retail the latest stories I glean from the wounded soldiers just in from the firing line? Some of these stories you would hardly believe, even though your little Flora absolutely vouches for them.

For instance, in the 1st Battalion there was one young Camelier who was a frightfully keen photographer. Scores of times he risked his life taking snaps during scraps. At Maghdaba, just as the front line—first wave, they called it—was getting ready to charge the redoubt, this wild harum-scarum yelled out to the officer, 'Half a mo!' and he rushed forward on his own, 20 yards or so, and fixed his camera. 'Righto!' he cried ; and as the yelling Cameliers came on he got a fine picture. Also he got a bullet in the leg which put him out of action for a couple of months.

But one of the most picturesque pictures of the campaign was when the Cameliers got into the Turkish trenches in the second battle of Gaza. They were the only unit in the British line to gain their objective. And they stuck to them in spite of repeated counter-attacks by the Turks, in the face of a hail of shells, and a devastating enfilade fire from machine guns. With the right not having come up, and the left held up after sustaining terrible casualties, the poor Cameliers were 'in the air'.

Abdul kept on attacking till sheer weight of numbers enabled him to fall on the last thirteen sundowners and capture them. As the unlucky baker's dozen were starting off as prisoners an adventurous pair ducked past the guards, leaped the parapet, and with bullets flying thick and fast around them, did a marathon for our trenches, 600 yards distant. As their cobbers rose in the trenches to cheer them in, they yelled frantically for beer and a ticket in Tatt's.

Digging in amidst a shower of bullets and shrapnel

opposite Gaza, one Anzac cavalier exclaimed, 'My Gord, I wish I was an ant.' Another scratching with his bayonet and scooping out with his hands at a tiny funk-hole, cried plaintively, 'Oh, why did I cut my nails this morning!' A third, as he gazed ruefully at a gaping wound in his shoulder, soliloquised, 'Cripes, it must ha' been an axe that stopped me, not a bullet.' Another, toppling over with a bullet in his knee, remarked judicially and without a trace of animosity, 'One to you, Abdul.' Many and varied are the exclamations of Billjim in the heat of battle; but on the eight hours' train-journey back to Kantara the crowds of wounded cried unanimously for 'Water, water, water!'

Chapter 17

The Soldier

After the two costly and abortive attacks on Gaza the I.C.C. settled down to the humdrum of trench warfare. They camped in and about the Wadi Ghuzzie, with the British infantry on their left and the cavalry on their right flank. There was but little excitement except the daily visits of the Hun 'planes, and in course of time even these daily strafes lost their savour.

The camels were eating their heads off, so the G.O.C. decided to give them something to do. One day when the enemy 'plane scouts had come and gone, and darkness had loomed up over the wadi, the Camel Brigade saddled up, and under cover of night moved back to Rafa. Few who participated in that trek will ever forget it. Early in the evening a blinding sand-storm swung up from Sinai. The west wind, charged with desert sand swept over the land with the force of a hurricane. The Cameliers coming back from the east got the full force of the storm in their teeth. The swirling sand lashed their faces. The poor camels instinctively swung round and had to be whipped forward. Surplus gear was ruthlessly jettisoned. The wind howled and played an aeolian dirge on the wires. At last, when every man's temper was ragged and every soldier's eyes, nose, mouth, and ears were full of grit, the cavalcade halted and bivouacked for the night.

Next morning early the unwashed, unshaven, bleary-eyed brigade resumed their trek and camped at Rafa. Here the camp had been so laid out that the battalions, and signallers, and gunners, and ambulance, and veterinarians, and headquarters were so far from each other that the enemy bombs could not possibly hit more than one unit at a time, and there was far more green sward to aim at than camel camps; which was fortunate, for the Taubes came over and bombed us, entirely ignoring the protecting fire of our 'Archies' and the salvos of the Bing Boys. However, Allah was kind, and the bombs for the most part ploughed up the innocent earth, and only managed to put on the casualty list one native and two camels.

A day or two later we started out for the Wadi Abiad. The scheme of the commander-in-chief was to smash up the railway line south-east of Beersheba, for the Turks were notoriously short of rolling-stock and rails. The victorious Desert Column was, of course, selected for the job. Major-General Chauvel was in charge of operations, and he took his cavalry and Light Horse and made a strong demonstration against Beersheba. The Turkish defences were shelled; the railway bridge north of the town was destroyed, and two enemy brigades of cavalry that came up were driven back home again. Under cover of this demonstration the special party of Light Horsemen and Engineers started on the railway line and made the whole length a wreck from Sadaj to Asluj. Fine stone bridges and culverts were blown up, and not a single rail left intact.

Meanwhile the Cameliers, without haste, without pause, had trekked southwards to El Auja. They travelled all night, and at dawn reached the Wadi Abiad, where they breakfasted. A long line of skirmishers then moved southwards over the line, scattered several Turkish patrols, and settled down ready for any attack, while the demolition party coming behind played havoc with the railway. For over an hour there sounded a continuous roar of detonations. Big railway bridges with solid stone and concrete pillars and arches all crashed and crumbled to ruin. Such is the waste and destruction incidental to the prosecution of war.

In the afternoon we drew off, and moved back to the Wadi Abiad to bivouac. Our aeroplane, which had kept us advised of Abdul's movements, landed near the old police posts of El Auja, but striking a bit of rough ground had the bad luck to bend the axle and break some minor parts. The pilot was unable to effect repairs without a forge and wires and special tools. It looked as if the machine would have to be destroyed to prevent it falling into the hands of the enemy. When the airman had about come to this decision, a couple of Cameliers sauntered up, had a look at the wreck, and reckoned they could patch it up somehow. The pilot was incredulous, but he said, "Go ahead." So they made a fire, heated and straightened the axle—using lumps of railway line for an anvil. They commandeered some telegraph wire, and soon had the aeroplane in working order again. The airman was delighted. So he got aboard again, waved a 'cheerio', and flew back to Rafa. Later on a special letter of thanks came from the Flight Commander to the bush carpenter who had effected the repairs, and they wondered why he should have made a fuss over such a little thing.

The Cameliers having had two nights in the saddle were mighty tired, so for the few hours vouchsafed them they slept without even taking their boots off. Before dawn we were on trek again, heading north for home. Here and there were Bedouin villages, and we tried to buy eggs and poultry and sheep; but the Bedouins did not want to trade with us. The boys cast covetous eyes on the sheep, but orders were that the property of the inhabitants was to be respected. So we thought of our bully beef and biscuits, and let the sheep pass unmolested—for the most part.

I say for the most part, for that night, as I munched my bully and biscuit, I detected a most savoury odour proceeding from our company lines. It was tantalising, aggravating in the extreme. I was fed up with bully beef anyhow. A few minutes later my section sergeant came along, dumped a delicious piece of roast lamb on my plate, and departed without a single word. I had learnt that pleasant mystery should simply be endured, so forbore to ask of sergeant where the mutton was procured. I just took a pinch of salt and pepper and waded in.

We had a couple of hours' sleep that night—and had earned them. Then once more it was saddle up before dawn and trek onward. We had left the sandy country behind us, and the going was excellent. The camels knew they were going home. The men were too sleepy to care. There had been a few shots fired at our rear-guard, but nobody worried. In due course we arrived back at Rafa. The usual 'furphy' had preceded us. It had been rumoured that we had been cut off and annihilated. We were hungry but happy at the prospect of a good night's sleep. So we gave our camels a drink—the first for five days—and were preparing to settle down for the night when orders came that we were to saddle up and trek back to Gaza.

Oh, what a roar was there, my countrymen. Tired troopers, having had scarcely any sleep for several days, lay all about the lines oblivious to everything. And here were they rudely awakened and ordered to saddle up. They grumbled and swore, and some fell asleep over the job. However, just at nightfall once more the league-long column straggled out of Rafa towards Gaza. No one cared now whither we were bound. Men were falling asleep, as they rode, and then falling off their camels. Several woke up next morning, only to find that their camels were gone on without them. Several times the column halted to rest the camels. Each time we dismounted and walked about and tried to remain awake. We trod on sleeping Cameliers, but they took no notice. We fell against our camels and slept. The camels didn't mind; they were too tired to care. We were rudely awakened as the camels rose up to follow the column.

That journey was one long nightmare. It seemed interminable. But at last, somewhere about three in the morning we heard someone say, "Rest for one hour." We just tumbled over where we were and slept.

It was dawn, with a rosy glow showing over the Eastern hills, when we were roused again. The larks were singing the morning hymn of praise. The poppies glowed red like drops of blood in the grass. Along the wadi thin spirals of smoke ascended heavenward. Evidently nothing startling had happened since we left. Away to the north was dimly heard the rumbling of artillery fire. We went back into our old dugouts in the Wadi Ghuzzie and slept and slept and slept. About midday someone called, "Mess orderlies". But no orderlies responded. No one woke to eat any dinner. Nobody cared.

From my dugout I could see a Taube sailing overhead with bursts of shrapnel all around. It never interested me in the slightest. For some inexplicable reason I was thinking of the "Ancient Mariner."

> *O sleep it is a gentle thing,*
> *Beloved from Pole to Pole.*
> *To Mary Queen the praise be given,*
> *She sent the blessed sleep from Heaven,*
> *That slid into my soul.*

I do not know if the lines are correct, but that is how, twenty years after I first had learnt them, the lines came again into my memory.

> *Nature's sweet restorer . . . sleep. . . .*

This demolition stunt of the Camelry formed the subject of the following parody on Mandalay published in *Barrak* :

Demolitions
Where the Turco-Gyppie frontier swings down south towards Akaba,
Where there ain't no Ten Commandments, and there ain't
    no motor-car,

Where the Camel Column straggles like a league-long desert snake,
There's a weeping Bedouin maiden, and she cries, "For Allah's sake,
Don't come back to Abiad,
Oh, the shocking time we had,
When your wild-eyed Camel soldiers smashed our railway
   awful bad.
On the road down Abiad,
Poor old Enver Pasha's mad,
And at dawn he swears like thunder, from Asluj to Abiad."

'Er petticoat—she 'ad none, and 'er dress was chocolat' tint,
We never knew her proper—she was just a Bedouin bint—
But we missed 'er baa-baa lambie when the Anzacs hurried by,
And all the long-night marches we could hear her plaintive cry:
"Don't come back to Abiad,
For the Turks are ragin' mad;
And tho' my lamb tastes better than the bully beef you've had.
Don't come back to Abiad.
Now you've gone I'm mighty glad,
For you rather wrecked El Auja when you trekked down Abiad."

Ship me somewhere west of Suez, where a bloke can get a sleep;
Where there ain't no blank Fray Bentos, and yer needn't
   pinch a sheep;
For my camel's getting dopey, and I cannot keep awake;
My bleary eyes are closing, and I pray, "For Heaven's sake,
Don't go back to Abiad,
For I need a snooze so bad;
Men are falling off their camels with a bump that sends them mad,
On the road to Abiad.
Oh, my humpy, grumpy prad,
You have brought me scathless, sleeping, from the Wadi Abiad."

Chapter 18

The Sister

Colonel Livingstone sat on the verandah of the old homestead, smoking his morning cigar and gazing across the fertile fields of Langlands. But his thoughts were far away—with the Hunter River boys in France and Sinai, but more particularly with his daughter in Egypt.

He seemed to live solely that he might read her letters, and Flora, knowing how lonely her old father must be, never let a week go by without writing home. Ever and anon the cowboy cantering along the river road with the mail-bag roused the old soldier from his reverie. A mail had arrived at Sydney from Egypt a few days before, so he knew there would be a letter from Flora.

My dear old Daddy—I'm fit and well, so don't worry your dear old head about your wayward spring-off. And I've been sent down lo the officers' ward, which is nicer in some ways. For instance, I've only been here a week, yet I've had three offers of marriage, four dinners at Shepheard's, and a trip on the Nile in a felucca. And I've got one dear little patient all to myself. He's just a mere boy; came in the other day with a shrapnel wound in his arm—stopped one while flying over Abdul's 'Archies'. He's in the Australian Flying Corps, and they are all heroes. I used to think the Australian Light Horse were the pick of the whole empire army, but I guess the airmen are a bit above them. Anyhow, about 80 per cent, of the Australian airmen in Sinai and Palestine are ex-Light Horsemen.

Do you know, Daddy, these knight-errants of the clouds have fought in every battle on this front since Romani. Oh, I do wish I could write a book about them! They've won about fifteen Military Crosses and a V.C. already. And they never think they are doing anything heroic. To them it's all a gorgeous adventure.

I suppose the unimaginative censor will cut this out, though the enemy knows it better than we do, but during the Sinai Campaign our poor boys had to do long reconnaissance patrols in old buses that could only do 60 miles per hour. The boys called them buses; the proper name is 2E.B.C. and 2E.B.E. My patient told me. Yet the Turks had beautiful fast Fokkers, and Albatross Scouts, and D.3's which were twice as fast and miles better fighting 'planes. But our boys never hesitated, and went up day after day. Sometimes they managed even in their old buses to drive Fritz off, but often they were chased home to Rafa or Sheikh Narran. Some never came back. (That's a blot and not a tear, Daddy.)

These cavalry of the clouds are all frightfully loyal to each other, and they risk anything rather than let their pals get into trouble. That was why M'Namara won his V.C. Dug Rutherford had to come to earth, through engine trouble, in the Turkish lines. The enemy cavalry were near, but M'Namara never hesitated. He zoomed down and had a look, then he alighted to take Rutherford up. But he struck a bad landing and broke his machine. He was wounded at the time, but he helped to fix the old machine and they both got in. Mac. took the air, and they both got away just as the Turks came up. It was awfully lucky.

But oh, Daddy, it's sad to think of the splendid young

fellows that have been killed, and for every one of them some mother or sister or sweetheart is breaking her heart. Already the Australian Flying Squadron has lost Steele and Jack Potts and Gerry Stone and Bowd,—we all loved Harry Bowd,—Paget, Searle, Harvey, Oxenham, Farquhar, Adams, and Muir. Muir was just splendid, and did some wonderful stunts before he was killed.

This is not a cheerful letter, is it, Daddy? But I must buck up. They do such comical things too, at times, these supermen. One chap was anxious to become a pilot. He went to Heliopolis to learn, and was landing after his first solus, when he crashed into the hangar and smashed his machine. The irate Flight Commander dashed out and yelled, 'You clumsy animal. That's the last time you'll fly here.' The culprit grinned, threw his cap, gloves, and overcoat to the mechanic, and said, 'Sir, I could have told you that.' Then he stalked off and went back to the Light Horse.

My airman tells me that the pilots and observers 'chiack' each other when they make a dud landing or anything. For instance, their champion bomber tried several times to blow up a Turkish pontoon over the Jordan, and though he got near it he just failed. He was very depressed with his failure, but the last straw was when an unofficial communique stated that when the Turks saw Haig's Horror coming to bomb it they rushed to the bridge for *safety* !

The officer in the next bed to my airman is a mining engineer, and he has been thousands of feet down big mines, and he has done a lot of sapping and tunnelling in this war. I asked him why he didn't join the Flying Corps; and he exclaimed emphatically, 'I'll go down, down as far as you like, but up? Not one blanky inch!'"... And I feel like that myself sometimes when I hear of the airmen's exploits.

Oh, I ought to tell you, Daddy, that whatever good sports there are in the German army seem to have gravitated to the Flying Corps. There is one chap named 'Filmy'. He's their star pilot. He has brought down several English and Australian airmen. One day after one of our chaps had been brought down 'Filmy' flew over our aerodrome, fired a Very light to show he had a message, dived down through our machines—which of course never attacked him—and dropped a message saying Vautin was all right, and that the Australian airmen were real good sports, and he hoped to meet some of them after the war.

I must stop, Daddy; I could write for hours and hours about the boys. The main thing is that since our airmen got the new Bristol Fighter Machines they have easily maintained the supremacy of the air. Frequently one or two of our boys will attack and disperse several Hun machines.

I've not told you much about the Camel Corps this time, have I? Well, now listen: 'I'm a bit fond of a big suntanned Camelier, somewhere in Palestine. So there.'
Your affectionate daughter,
Flora

It was a curious coincidence that just as the old Colonel finished reading his daughter's letter he picked up the *Sydney Morning Herald,* and in it read the following account by a Camelier of the doings of the Australian airmen in Sinai and Palestine:

Airmen, birdmen, fliers, pilots, observers, kings of the air—heroes all:

We ordinary soldiers of *terra firma*, horse, foot, artillery, and camelry—we salute you!

In the good old days when the world was wide our fathers fought on land and sea. Today Armageddon is so vast that men needs must fight above the land and under the water as well, and those who still follow the prosaic paths on land and sea look up and wonder or look down and ponder.

I have flown. For a brief space, one glorious hour—or maybe less—I shared in the kingship of the air. I have mounted up with wings like an eagle, and breathed the rarefied air of the high places. Tomorrow, and the next day, and the next, I will ride a camel, breathe dust, live in sand, drink lukewarm water, and eat bully beef and biscuits. But today I have been aloft and looked down on the dwellers on the earth.

The first phase is just like a wild rush in an automobile. The 'plane streaked across the ground at about twenty or thirty miles an hour, and aimed straight at a huge hangar. It looked absolutely certain that we must crash into the building. Then it seemed a miracle happened, and we leapt into space. The pilot had just touched a lever, and the machine, spurning the ground, cleared the hangar and floated away into the rosy dawn. Farther and farther receded the earth. Trees dwindled till they became little smudges. Trenches thinned until they looked like irregular lines disfiguring the landscape. The horizon momentarily widened. For miles and miles the vast panorama stretched away and below—green fields, golden sands, blue shimmering waters, one great Cyclopean picture. The tents of the soldiers looked like little whitey brown drops of paint. The blankets laid out on the ground to air were just like tiny black, brown, and grey patches, one-eighth the size of a pocket-handkerchief. 'Way out in the open is a long string of little grey ants at least they look like ants; in reality they are camels. How the airmen must look down on the poor Cameliers!

We circled and banked; flew before the breeze at anything over a hundred miles an hour. Facing the wind again the 'plane throbbed and quivered; swerving and swooping as we encountered various air currents or pockets. Then the whirring engine suddenly ceased. We poised like an eagle with outstretched wings. Anon, the 'plane tilted forward, and with incredible velocity we rushed earthwards. The distant horizon dropped out of sight. Bigger and bigger grew the tents and the camels and the trenches. A little toy train some miles off assumed quite respectable dimensions. Up, up, up came the earth to meet us. Soon we could distinguish the Lilliputian soldiers. A breathless swoop, one final exhilarating rush through the air, and we were once more safe on *terra firma*.

Let it be at once admitted that this was no dare-devil flight over the enemy's lines, with its attendant dangers from 'Archies' and Taubes. It was just a simple 'joy ride' right back in the safety of our own territory. But the experience only served to heighten the admiration I had always felt for our intrepid airmen. Some days before, I had been the guest of the Australian Flying Squadron at Rafa. It had been good day after day watching those courageous pilots taking their machines out, executing fancy flights overhead, and then streaking east for the daily duel with the Hun. Now it was fine to see them at close quarters, when the day's work was over, happy and care-free as a party of schoolboys. Indeed, the first thing noticed was the extreme youth of the majority of the airmen. They seemed all to be within the enviable twenty to twenty-five period. There was not a middle-aged man amongst the lot of them, and hardly a man over thirty. They were really just a party of big boys engaged in a great game.

Each day brought its attendant excitement: a flight over Abdul's lines, a brief and thrilling duel with a Hun, a bombing expedition anywhere between Gaza and Jerusalem; perhaps a forced landing on account of engine troubles, or maybe a hilarious rush to funk-holes when the Hun airmen paid the return visit. Then when the day's 'strafe' was over the airmen lounged about the mess, reading or smoking or sleeping. And at night they fought their battles over again—not in a spirit of bravado, but that all might know all that was going on, and profit by the experience of the day. The airmen have a jargon of their own, and it takes the uninitiated some time to gauge the import of their vernacular. And some of their exploits are enough to make one's hair stand on end. A few of the more spectacular deeds now and then find their way into the cable columns of the papers. But for the most part very little is heard of the airmen's doings.

There seems to be such a lot of luck—good and bad—in the air fighting. A bullet in the petrol tank, a mishap with the engine, makes all the difference between plus and minus. The other day our Cameliers saw a thrilling duel aloft. A Hun and a Briton entered the lists. They were only a few thousand feet up, but being close together the 'Archies' could not open fire. So Turks and Anzacs looked on. The pilots circled and manoeuvred for position. At last the red and blue circle managed to get over the Taube, which promptly bolted. Then like an eagle the Briton swooped, blazing away with his machine gun at the flying Hun. It looked a certainty that the German must be riddled with bullets and brought crashing down. Then luck stepped in. The unexpected happened. Something went wrong with the British 'plane. The wings buckled, and like a wounded bird it swerved, dipped, then crashed to earth a shapeless mass. The report should have been: 'We brought down one enemy 'plane today.' Alas, it read: 'One, of ours failed to return.'

CHAPTER 19

Allenby—1

When Sir Edmund Allenby arrived in Egypt at the end of June 1917, things were anything but bright. The British army, twice hurled back with heavy slaughter from the heights of Gaza, had taken up a position extending for 22 miles from the Mediterranean Sea opposite Gaza to Gamlie. The midsummer sun seemed to focus all his rays on the Wadi Ghuzzie, and the tired infantry sweated and swore and prayed to get back to France.

Out towards Beersheba and Hareira the Light Horse and Cameliers played poker and two-up, and when a newcomer grumbled about the heat they grinned and shrugged their shoulders, and exclaimed "Maleesch!" So to relieve the monotony the Hun 'planes came on moonlight nights and bombed the bivouacs. Incidentally they deliberately bombed the hospitals and killed several of our wounded. And when the medical officers lit flares to show up the Red Cross, the Huns swooped down and loosed off a few thousand rounds from machine guns. Oh, there is nothing half-hearted about the Hun. He is as thorough as Stafford. It was not a cheerful prospect for the new commander-in-chief. The enemy occupied an almost impregnable position stretching from Gaza to Beersheba. Gaza itself, with its protecting redoubts, had been converted into a fortress. Earthworks and redoubts at intervals along the Beersheba

Road commanded all approaches. On a front of about 30 miles Marshal von Falkenhayn had disposed an army of 200,000 men, including German and Austrian gunners, machine gunners, and cavalry.

But it was not long before a new spirit of optimism animated our whole army. Allenby's genius, his enthusiasm, his energy permeated everywhere. The Expeditionary Force settled down manfully to prepare for the strenuous days ahead. The soldiers knew that when all was ready Allenby would strike, but not an hour before; and when he did strike they knew he would strike hard.

The 1st Battalion I.C.C., having borne the brunt of the Sinai Campaign, Romani, Rafa, and Maghdaba, and having been badly cut up in the second battle of Gaza, were now sent down to the Suez Canal for a few months' spell. The 4th Battalion, heartily sick of the scorching sands of Sinai, were brought up to the Wadi Ghuzzie in their stead. Later on there was a change in the command of the 4th. The commanding officer returned to Australia. The 4th hailed with unfeigned delight the news that Lieut.-Colonel Mills was to command. Lieut.-Colonel Mills won the whole-souled devotion of his men, and he in turn had implicit confidence in them. "They'll do me," he had exclaimed with pride at his first battalion parade. And the men, reciprocating, said, "He'll do us." Which was very satisfactory all round. When summer had done its worst, and the cool winter nights were freshening up the men, there was a general stir which presaged a renewal of the conflict. Abdul knew the blow was coming, but he could not guess when or where. With a view of finding out something of our dispositions he made a strong reconnaissance towards Karm, employing in the venture a couple of regiments of cavalry, some guns, and about three battalions of infantry. This force managed to mop up a couple of Yeomanry outposts, though it cost them very dear. Then the Welsh Division swung into action and the Turks bolted back to their trenches on the Gaza-Beersheba Road.

At the second battle of Gaza, the British commander had presumed that the Turkish left-flank trenches and works put any encircling movement by our cavalry out of the question. So the infantry were given the almost impossible task of capturing by frontal attack a series of redoubts bristling with machine guns. General Allenby's appreciation of the situation was different. He realised the cost of a frontal attack and the advantages of a flank attack. So he just chopped Beersheba off the left of the Turkish line. This left their flank exposed. He then hurled his cavalry and camelry on to the exposed left flank of the enemy, crumpled it up, and disorganised the Turks' whole plan of defence. Gaza fell.

The first phase, then, was the capture of Beersheba. Strategy dictated this, as well as the urgent necessity for supplementing the water supply. All through the campaign the water problem was acute. Besides the army there were 30,000 camels and thousands of horses and mules to be watered.

It was vitally important that the enemy should not guess from which direction the main attack was coming. The artillery therefore opened a three days' bombardment of the whole Turkish position, and on the third day the warships under Rear-Admiral Jackson joined in the chorus and directed destructive salvos at the works round Gaza. Under cover of night the Light Horse, Camel Corps, Artillery, and London and Welsh Infantry congregated at the rendezvous within striking distance of Beersheba.

The Beersheba battle began with the Londoners dashing forward at dawn and seizing the Turks' advanced position. Incidentally they killed a goodly number of the enemy and captured a hundred more. This enabled the guns to push forward and tear the wire entanglements to smithereens. All the preliminaries being satisfactorily accomplished, the Camels attacked the defences to northward. Cavalry threatened the south and east, while the main advance from the west by British infantry resulted in the capture of the positions between the Khalusa Road and the Wadi Saba. This took till midday; the enemy artillery, being exceptionally active, did some execution among the troops advancing in the open. A force encircling the town attacked the strongly fortified Tel el Saba and Bir es Sakaty, but met with a stout resistance. Meanwhile the Australian Light Horse, having ridden 35 miles during the night, swung in towards Beersheba from the east. The steady advance by platoons of infantry over the open was too slow for their liking, so with a wild yell they charged straight for the town. It was quite unorthodox, considering the force holding the defences, but it was eminently successful. It was a surprise packet. It decided the day. Like steeple-chasers the Anzacs cleared two lines of deep trenches and galloped right into the town. Turks surrendered wholesale. This happened just about seven in the morning, so the demoralised Turks never knew how many foe-men were amongst them. The Yeomanry and Londoners charging from the west gave the garrison no chance to recover from their panic. The ancient city of Abraham, with its wells and precious water supply, was captured with comparatively slight loss to the British. At least 500 Turks were killed and 2000 captured. A dozen cannon and a vast quantity of ammunition and stores were gathered as spoils to the victors. This was Allenby's first step on the road to Jerusalem.

The following tribute to the Light Horsemen—in the *Melbourne Herald*—is worth quoting:

"These Light Horsemen that night carried through by endurance, grit, and fine horsemanship, one of the great feats of the war ... a brilliant feat of arms. No better cavalry have existed. The great ride of the Australians and New Zealanders to Beersheba outdid Stewart's long dashes in the American Civil War and French's rounding-up work in South Africa."

It was round Beersheba that 'Tibbie' Cotter the cricketer was killed, with many more Light Horsemen and Cameliers. There are rough wooden crosses dotting the land of the Philistines. Some bear the names of comrades; some are nameless.

Comrade of knapsack or bandolier,
Tread light, we pray, when you pass this way;
For sake of the brave one slumbering here,
Nameless in death till the Judgement Day:
Tread light, lest the tramp of your martial host
Or the rattle of rifle or bayonet blade
Should ring down the night to their silent post,
And rouse them too soon for the Grand Parade.

Chapter 20

Allenby—2

Our army was now in great heart. The optimism of October had developed into an absolute certainty of victory. Beersheba had been bitten off. The Turks' left flank lay exposed, and they were feverishly hastening the supplementary defences round Khuweilfeh and Sheria.

It was, however, still essential that they should remain in ignorance of the next move. The scene of operations was therefore suddenly shifted from their extreme left at Beersheba to their extreme right at Sheikh Hasan and Umbrella Hill. These two works are only about 2000 to 2500 yards from the town, so their capture would be a distinct menace to Gaza itself. It was also hoped that an assault here would pin the Turkish reserves to the town and prevent them reinforcing the threatened left flank.

Umbrella Hill was first essayed. The Lowland Scotties moved out over the heavy sand-hills at night on 1st November. It was heavy going and stiff fighting on arrival, but there was no doubt of the result. To show their anger at the loss of the 'Gamp', the Turks opened a violent two hours' bombardment of our line, and also plastered Umbrella Hill. Then at three o'clock on 2nd November the attack was hurled at the enemy's right. After a heavy preliminary bombardment the British infantry moved out, and in splendid style captured the 5000 yards of trenches comprising the Sheikh Hasan position. Our left was now firmly settled on the seashore. The bombardment had caused many casualties among the Gaza garrison, while the infantry landed 450 prisoners, apart from killed and wounded. What was more important, the Turkish commander had not dared to deplete his reserves to reinforce his exposed left flank.

Out here—the Turks' left—the Welsh and Irish infantry, with the cavalry and camelry on their wing, were threatening Sheria and beginning the work of crumpling up the line. It was no easy task. The whole line had been strongly fortified, while trenches, pits, and barbed wire provided obstacles against the cavalry. The Irish Division moved up and captured Abu Irgey. The Welsh pushed on through the hills north of Beersheba and attacked Sheria on the flank. The Cameliers on the right of the Welsh pushed on to Khuweilfeh. The Anzac Mounteds moved north along the Hebron Road towards Dhaheriyeh. By 3rd November a concerted movement by Irish, Welsh, and Colonials, north and west towards Sheria and Khuweilfeh, made plain the British strategy. The path was strenuously contested by the Turkish garrison, and strong reserves were hurried from Gaza to save the left flank. Here some of the hottest fighting of the campaign took place. Time and again for three days the Turks counter-attacked the Cameliers and Light Horse and the Welsh. Here it was that Lieut. Dixon of the Anzac Camelry won his D.S.O. and his captaincy, by rallying some scattered infantry and I.C.C., and with a mere handful of men barring the road against repeated charges of the enemy.

Fighting in this sector was fierce and indecisive for a couple of days. The Welsh by a brilliant charge captured Khuweilfeh, but a counter-attack drove them off. They came again with undiminished ardour, retook the hill, and went on. Then on the 6th the main attack on the Turkish left centre was driven home. Yeomanry, Irish, Londoners, Welsh, Australians, and New Zealanders converged from the south and east on Abu

Hareira, Wadi Sheria, Kanwukah, Khuweilfeh, and Rijin el Dhib. Behind them the artillery thundered away at the redoubts and the Turkish batteries. On the left of this sector the Yeomanry charged the hills and stormed the redoubt with magnificent valour, taking several lines of trenches and reaching the Sheria Station, with a bag of 600 Turks to their credit. On the right the Welsh had another strenuous day's fighting, from which they emerged victorious, having captured several hundred more prisoners. For four days the Camel Corps had sustained the shock of successive battalions of Turkish reinforcements, holding the ground manfully, and by using up the army's resources made possible the victory in the centre. But their casualties had been heavy. Hardly a company could put fifty men in the firing line. Sections had dwindled to about a dozen men. But they stuck it.

The commander-in-chief had wisely refrained from frittering away his reserves, trusting to the right sector to carry out its own job. Thus, on the night of 6-7th November he was able to concentrate for the final blow at Outpost Hill, Middlesex Hill, and Turtle Hill, immediately in front of Gaza. The artillery once more pounded away at the defences, and the infantry started out to finish the job. But Abdul didn't wait. With Beersheba captured, Gaza itself threatened, his left flank turned, and his line crumbling up, he made a second getaway. Gaza had fallen at last!

CHAPTER 21

Allenby—3

The third battle of Gaza made ample amends for the failures of 26th March and 19th April. All the energies of the 'C.-in-C.' were now concentrated on driving home the victory, and preventing the enemy taking up further defensive positions farther north.

When the main defences of Gaza had been occupied, a force was immediately pushed on to the mouth of the Wadi Hesi. Here the Turkish rear-guard temporarily held up pursuit. Away on the right, round Sheria, the enemy held on daring the 7th, but that night they joined the great trek northwards. Our airmen, during the 7th and 8th, made good practice with bombs and machine guns amongst the retreating enemy. The whole British army, from Beersheba to the sea, moved on. Every now and then the pursuing columns were checked for a brief time by small parties of Turks with machine guns fighting scattered rear-guard actions. Hareira and Sheria were captured at the point of the bayonet, and the Mounteds pushed on towards Jemaminah and Huj. At the latter place a more determined stand was made by the rear-guard, but the Warwick and Worcester Yeomanry made a fine spectacular charge, routing the enemy and capturing amongst the booty 12 field guns.

But for the lack of water and the difficulty of bringing up supplies, the retreat would have developed into an absolute rout. As it was, the cavalry pushed on relentlessly, driving the foe before them. Prisoners were surrendering wholesale all along the line. There had been only nine days of fierce fighting, yet a modern army nearly a quarter of a million strong had been driven from an almost impregnable fortress and was in full retreat. It was surely a nine days' wonder.

There was, however, no easing up and resting on the laurels already won. An ordinary soldier may win a battle, but it takes a military genius to reap the full fruits of victory. And this is what General Allenby was bent on doing. The mounted troops were assembled, and with scarcely a pause pushed on after the enemy. The main Turkish army had retreated north along the plain towards Jaffa, while the considerable force that had held Sheria and the Hareira positions had made a more leisurely get-away towards Menshiye. In fact, at one time the position of this force constituted a menace to the right wing of the main pursuing British army. An undefeated army well in hand might have caused considerable trouble by a determined attack westward along the Wadi Hesi, behind our advancing troops. But all the fight had been taken out of Abdul. He was useless for any strategical move. The most he could do was to fight spasmodic rear-guard actions. It would have needed Marshal Ney at his best to hold up the British advance. But in case any flank attack did come from the hills, the Camel Corps was pushed on towards Nijile, while the Anzac Mounted Division hung pitilessly on the right rear, hustling the rear-guards, cutting in on detached bodies, capturing hundreds of prisoners, and transforming the retreat into a rout.

By 11th November the main Turkish army was moving on Junction Station. By strenuous labours the German Staff had been able to rally about 20,000 men. The main army on the plain had outdistanced the force retreating through the Judæan hills, so the line of resistance stretched in a general south-east direction from Wadi Sukereir on the coast *via* El Kustineh towards Beit Jebrin. So for a brief space the pursuing British had perforce to halt while the men and horses rested, and to enable supplies to come forward.

It had been terribly strenuous work. Although nominally winter, it was very warm during the day. Hot wind and dust inflicted severe thirst on the troops, and water was very scarce. At night in the hills it was bitterly cold.

There had been intermittent fighting on 11th and 12th November. On the right of our line the Australians and New Zealanders, giving the hapless Turks no rest, had pushed on and driven the rear-guards back to Balin and Tel es Safi. On the other flank the cavalry and Lowlanders had pushed the enemy back towards Nahr Sukereir and Burkah. So on the 13th the Turks had taken up a very strong semi-circular position defending the all-important Junction Station, whence the line runs east to Jerusalem and north to Ramleh.

Once more the victorious army got ready for attack. Supplies were brought up and a few guns ranged in support. Then once again Allenby hurled his troops at the enemy. Round Katrah and El Mughar the strong natural position had been strengthened by the defenders, and there was stiff fighting before the Scotties won home. The Anzacs on the right drove back the Turkish left, while the cavalry, by a magnificent charge from the north-west, broke through the last defences, sabring all who disputed their path. Falkenhayn's proud army was cut in two, half fleeing north towards the coast and the remainder making all haste east to Jerusalem.

CHAPTER 22

Allenby—4

Some day the full story will be written of Allenby's Palestine Campaign—one of the most brilliant and decisive campaigns in history. Historians will do justice to the English, Scots, Irish, Welsh, Indian, Australian, and New Zealand Divisions engaged in the great enterprise. These few chapters, written near the banks of the old Jordan River, provide a very sketchy and imperfect resume of the victorious progress of Allenby's army.

Nor does it profess to present more than occasional vignettes of that truly imperial force, the Imperial Camel Corps. In the fighting which began at Beersheba and ended at Jerusalem on 9th December, the Cameliers claim—not very seriously—that they fasted for forty days and forty nights. Which, of course, is an exaggeration; yet it gives an inkling of the hardships which the whole army must have suffered, for the Cameliers are the last to go short of tucker. Ordinarily we marched out with five days' rations and water aboard, and time and again this supply had to be shared with the less fortunate cavalry and infantry. Out on the western desert, during the fighting with the Senussi, Light Horsemen and infantry often besieged the Camel Corps, offering pound notes for bottles of water, but no matter how long the trek or how distant the next supply, the Cameliers always gladly placed their fantasses at the disposal of their comrades.

During the campaign under review, the Camel brigade, under Brigadier-General Smith, V.C., M.C., was represented by one Australian battalion, one Anzac battalion, one British battalion, two Indian batteries, besides Engineers, Army Medical Corps, and details. This Imperial brigade, working mostly on the right of the line, formed the connecting link between the infantry and the mounted troops, and the pivot upon which the cavalry swung when attacking the flank of the enemy. Some of the hottest fighting round Khuweilfeh fell to their lot, and throughout the entire forty days they co-operated loyally with the Welsh and other infantry with whom they were associated. It will be remembered that by 13th November the demoralised Turkish army had been defeated near Junction Station, and cut in two, the main force still retreating north towards Jaffa, and the remainder making along the line to Jerusalem. Once more the British pushed on in pursuit. The successive though sacrificial rear-guard actions had indeed enabled the main army to effect a get-away, but it was a demoralised and beaten force. As they neared Jaffa, however, a last effort was made to hold up the pursuit. A strong line was chosen south of Ramleh, the right resting on Ayun Kara, and the left fining the ridge at Ancient Gezer, which covers the main Ramleh-Jerusalem Road. Without hesitation this defence was attacked on 15th November. The cavalry swinging up from the south charged the Gezer heights and brilliantly carried the position, capturing several hundred prisoners and a field gun. On the Mediterranean wing the New Zealand Mounted Rifles found the Turks strongly entrenched, but the irresistible dash of the Colonials carried the heights. The Turks came again with a determined counter-attack, driving the New Zealanders back.

Once again the New Zealanders scaled the hill with fixed bayonets. The Turks met them fair and square—one of the few occasions when Abdul has dared to meet the Anzac in the open with the cold steel. A wild *mêlée* ensued, the cries of the Turks mingling with the wild yells of the Maorilanders. But in spite of their numerical superiority and the frenzied exhortations of the German officers, the Turks were no match for the Anzacs at close quarters. They broke and fled, leaving many killed behind, and Ayun Kara in possession of the New Zealanders.

Throughout the whole Sinai and Palestine Campaigns, from Romani onwards, the New Zealanders had been conspicuously successful. They had suffered the most intense privations with the utmost cheerfulness. Their charge was always irresistible. The Australian Light Horsemen, who had shared the rigours of the campaign with them, were supposed to be rather jealous of their own reputation. Yet I heard at Jericho an English staff officer, who ought to know, exclaim, "The New Zealanders are absolutely the pick of the whole Palestine army," and the Australians, without hesitation or dissentient voice, heartily agreed. After the victory at Ayun Kara and Abu Shusheh the army pushed on, and the mounted troops and Cameliers occupied Ramleh and Ludd. Next day they pushed on, and without hindrance entered Jaffa. Towards Jerusalem there was some fierce fighting round the Judæan Hills. Infantry with Australian Light Horse on their flank rooted guerilla fighters out from amongst the wadis and denies. But the German machine gunners now made some amends for their long retreat. They seized all the vantage-posts on the hills. They commanded all the approaches, even the goat-tracks. The British, storming the heights, suffered considerable casualties, but after a brief spell for relief on 4th December pushed on to the north of Jerusalem. Round Nebi Samwil and El Burg and El Toka there were fierce fighting and repeated counter-attacks by the Turks, but all to no avail. On the coast round Jaffa most determined counter-attacks were made by the enemy from 25th November to 1st December. Time and again they charged our lines. For eleven days the Cameliers dared not take the saddles off their unfortunate camels. Hardly any grain or fodder had come up to feed them. The Light Horsemen were almost continuously in the saddle. Fighting was fierce and incessant. On 29th November the Turks charged in force, and 150 were promptly surrounded and mopped up by the Australians. Again, at El Burge on the extreme right a mass attack resulted in a serious break through, but here again the Australian Light Horse counter-attacked with brilliant success, killing many Turks, driving the wedge back, restoring the line, and capturing over 200 prisoners.

Then came the final move on Jerusalem. Roads were constructed, guns were brought up, water supplies were developed, and troops set in motion. Then came the rain. The roads became impassable for wheeled transport and camels. Difficulties of transport and manoeuvre and signalling were increased tenfold. But through the mud and slush and mire the troops pushed on. Camels slithered over the slippery hill-track and broke their legs. Motors could not move. But the army moved on. Rations failed to arrive. But the infantry went on without them. The Australians raided the orchards, paying whatever was asked so long as they got tucker. And an unlimited supply of oranges saved the situation. In due course Jerusalem was surrounded and the Turks retreated northwards.

On 9th December, without a shot being fired at its walls, the ancient city surrendered.

CHAPTER 23

Allenby—5

Allenby has entered Jerusalem. Another conqueror has passed through the walls of the ancient city.

But the glory has departed from the city of David. Gone are its pristine splendour, its prosperous days, its thriving commerce, its gorgeous bazaars, its thronging pilgrims. War and misrule have sorely tried the Holy City; famine and disease have cowed the unfortunate citizens.

It has been said that where the Red Sultan merely lashed the Jews with whips, the Young Turks had flayed them with scorpions. Commerce was only possible when the merchants heavily bribed the Turkish officials. Being a non-producing city, the citizens lived an artificial life, based on the gold left in the wake of the constant stream of pilgrims. But when war came the pilgrimage ceased. The main source of supply was cut off. The sole industry—that of manufacturing and selling souvenirs and relics and curios—languished and died. Soon shops and eating-houses became fewer and fewer. Famine and pestilence were rife. The young men were conscripted for military service. All over the city, shops and houses were shut and deserted. The evil days had come upon the city.

Remittances from abroad kept many of the Jews from starvation. But the iniquitous Turkish officials received the full value, American and British, and paid out the depreciated Turkish note, thus robbing the unfortunate inhabitants of 75 per cent, of their remittances. Then came the sound of guns, and hope fluttered in the breasts of the sorely-tried citizens. Anon the streams of Turkish fugitives passed through and on to Nablus. The German Staff in haste gathered their treasure and fled, and to the relief of all, and the joy of most, the British came; and after four centuries of tyranny and misrule the Ottoman dominion came to an end. Many times has the city of David seen the conflict of armies and the invasion of conquerors, but there was none like the present. Though the Turkish guns fired from the Mount of Olives and the sacred hills round the city, no British bullet or shell was turned in its direction.

On 9th December the city was surrendered, what time the diminishing firing showed that the Turks were being driven north and east from its walls. Next day General Allenby entered the city. But he came not with pomp and panoply and egotistic ceremonial, like the Hun pseudo-conqueror twenty years before. With a small staff and representative units of the Imperial army, he formally entered the city. He came on foot, not by the Joppa Gate, nor by the presumptuous breach made by the Hun, but by the ancient gate known as 'The Friend', and the citizens welcomed the deliverer with tears of joy.

The ceremony was brief but impressive. The procession marched from Mount Zion to the citadel, and at the base of the Tower of David the proclamation was read. It promised liberty to all to carry on legitimate commerce and industry. It assured the protection of every shrine, mosque, and sacred building, according to its own religious customs and practices, and the freedom of worship to all. After this simple ceremony General Allenby formally received the city notables, the patriarchs of the various religious denominations, and the leading sheikhs.

The spectacular victories of General Allenby, followed by his simple yet dignified entry into Jerusalem, have appealed to the imagination of the Arabs. Scarcely less potent a factor in securing the loyalty of the Arabs is the General's name. The Arabic Alla-nebi means 'The prophet of God.' Scholars have translated All-en-by as meaning 'God lodges with us', while read backwards, as in the Arabic, the name implies 'The servant of Allah'. And coming into the city on foot as he did, the Arabs have called him 'The Pilgrim'.

So a new era has dawned for the Holy City. Trade is livening up. Stores and bazaars and eating-houses are opening. There are life and movement in the air. The blight of the Turk and the menace of the Hun are now things of the past. The German Staff never thought the big British push had sufficient momentum to carry the invaders much farther north than the neighbourhood of Gaza. But they came on and on and on, and the Turks and their masters went back and back and back. Still the Huns believed that General Allenby could not hold Jerusalem. To show their confidence, they entered into a big wheat deal, the grain to be available a fortnight from date, by which time the British would certainly be driven back from Jerusalem. Reinforcements were hurried down from Damascus, and the big counter-attack launched against the tired British army. But, contrary to Hun expectations, the hated English had not lost their punch. They stood firm, while the Turks spent their fury in wild but hopeless charges. Then Allenby pushed on again, and the only effect of the attempted recapture of Jerusalem was to lose more Turkish territory.

And so the old war-scarred year ended with Southern Palestine freed from the Turkish yoke, and antipodean Colonials walking proudly through the streets of the Holy City. Colonel Todd and his Westralians were the first in, and surely their splendid record from Gallipoli to Jerusalem entitled them to the honour.

The Jews in the city looked thin and half starved; so much so, that a casual sand-groper, remembering his Old Testament, exclaimed, "No wonder it took two of them to carry a bunch of grapes." And his comrade in the same strain remarked, "Old

Moses was wise all right. He had one good look at this country, then pegged out."

There was, however, no doubt of the satisfaction of the populace at the British occupation. With tears of joy they welcomed "The Deliverer". Some months before—after the second battle of Gaza—when British prisoners were taken through Jerusalem, the people cheered the captives, and for this demonstration were punished vindictively by the Germans. But now German prisoners were marched through, and the people came out to feast their eyes on the spectacle and revile their old-time persecutors.

British Colonial statesmanship is constructive, in striking contrast to the destructive incidence of Turkish misrule. So it was not long before British Engineers were busily engaged laying water-pipe lines to Jerusalem. And when the citizens found the ever-flowing stream at their doors, instead of relying on the old-time cisterns, they marvelled. One Armenian priest with tears in his eyes exclaimed, "The Turks held Jerusalem for hundreds of years and gave us nothing; the English have been here a few months and they have given us a permanent water supply. Long live England!" Somehow, I think, that prayer finds an echo in the hearts of all the peoples of Palestine.

Chapter 24

The Soldier

Among the various institutions which have catered for the army of Egypt, not a single one in any way compares in excellence with the Y.M.C.A. The maps of Egypt, Sinai, Sudan, and Palestine are dotted with Red Triangle huts, scores of them, each one a boon and a blessing to the soldiers, a home of healthful recreation and a needful centre of social and spiritual activities.

These Y.M.C.A. huts, tents, and canteens are so much an integral part of the army organisation that one shudders to think what the E.E.F. would have been without them. The regimental padres have done noble work, yet I dare maintain that without the inspiring influence of the Y.M.C.A. the morale of the army would have sagged, the communications with home would have been much more precarious, and the vitiating influences of camp life, unchecked, would have seriously affected the efficiency of the troops.

Once freed from the irksome restraints of camp routine the average soldier is only too glad to throw himself down in his bivvy and smoke or play cards. It is quite an effort to write home. Besides, paper and envelopes are scarce. And it is so easy to procrastinate. So the thoughtless soldier goes on day after day, and week after week—always intending to write home, but always putting it off. Then he saunters into the Y.M.C.A. tent, and staring him in the face is the imperative injunction:"Write Home *Now.*" Paper and envelopes and pen and ink lie invitingly on the table. The careless soldier is filled with remorse. He did not mean to be cruel to the old folks at home. He was only thoughtless and tired and fed-up with the war. So he sits down and writes and writes and writes. Then in a month or so, way back in the Hunter River Valley, or in the Riverina, or in the Darling Downs, or out in the Never-Never Country, some mother or sister or sweetheart is gladdened by a letter from the wanderer. In one month in one camp alone 80,000 sheets of paper and 70,000 envelopes were used by the soldiers.

Owing to the exigencies of the military situation large bodies of men are transferred from time to time from one camp to another. Someone in Cairo or Rafa or Kantara writes a few orders, then, with the rapidity of the prophet's gourd, a canvas town springs up, maybe in the wilderness. Thousands of men are congregated together. It is necessary that someone should cater for their physical, social, mental, and spiritual needs. So in due course a Y.M.C.A. hut or tent is erected. A canteen is started, and the crowds of patrons testify to the need. Then someone else in authority writes more orders, and the battalion or brigade moves out to the front line. The camp is deserted. So the Y.M.C.A. packs up its impedimenta and follows the army. Tel el Kebir was once a great camp with tens of thousands of Anzacs. Six months later a few tired soldiers gazed on a beggarly array of empty huts. Mena at the end of 1914 was the home of the immortal 1st Australian Division. A year or so later the Sphinx and the Pyramids stood sentinel over a deserted landscape.

So the Y.M.C.A. is ever on the move. When the Sinai Campaign developed and a big army moved along the old caravan route from Kantara to Gaza, no fewer than 59 new Y.M.C.A. centres were opened in one year. The army pushed on, and 44 of these centres had to be abandoned. There was no one left to cater for. So in the course of three years 120 different Y.M.C.A. centres were established. Many of these were short-lived. A few are permanent, most of them moved on. As I write there are about 70 in active operation, extending from Khartoum to Jaffa and Jericho. The work centres in Cairo, and it is good for the moral and physical welfare of the soldiers that this is so. It is difficult to estimate the value to the army of the Anzac Hostel, but its space is limited to about 550. It is always well patronised and often crowded. In March 1916 the Y.M.C.A. took over the hostel, and it has been a godsend. The concerts there are crowded with grateful soldiers down from the front line. When one remembers the many distractions and temptations of Cairo, the work of the hostel is beyond all praise.

Right in the centre of Cairo are the Esbekiyeh Gardens—a cool and refreshing haven from the dust and heat of the city. Here among the trees and flowers and purling fountains the soldier finds recreation and rest. Last year the daily average attendance at the Esbekiyeh Y.M.C.A. was over 1500. There is an open-air concert stage, buffet, reading-and-writing room, roller-skating rink, and an inquiry bureau. This centre has been about three years in operation and deserves well of the army and of the Empire.

All over Sinai and Palestine I have encountered the Red Triangle; its ramifications are extraordinary. The canteen work alone is a great business enterprise. In Cairo and Alexandria tens of thousands of convalescents have been entertained at concerts, sports, and sight-seeing, and with refreshments. And the little Y.M.C.A. tents and marquees follow the men right up to the firing line, where they are most needed, where the everlasting bully beef and biscuits are hated cordially, and where a change of diet, got from the canteen, is thrice welcome. Once, out near the Wadi Ghuzzie, after the second battle of Gaza, I stumbled across a heap of stores dumped unceremoniously on the plain, and near by was the Y.M.C.A. secretary selling his stock to clamorous Cameliers and hungry Light Horsemen.

Do battle and the imminence of death make men more religious? The question has often been asked. It is difficult to gauge the thoughts of others and presumptuous to pretend to portray the soul of the soldier. Yet I dare affirm that battle makes no noticeable difference to the average Australian soldier. He goes laughing or singing or swearing into battle just as he goes about his ordinary work. So I am inclined to answer the question in the negative. After battle there is an obvious sense of relief and gratitude for coming out scathless, but it is rarely expressed. Still one *feels it*.

Does camp life tend to improve men, or the reverse? This question also is often asked. Admittedly war brings out the best and the worst in men. The one great act of patriotism and self-sacrifice would seem to more than compensate for all minor faults and failings. So when the Australian soldier—purely a volunteer—first goes into camp, he has made the great decision and offered his life for his country and freedom. It is his great hour of self-sacrifice; he is at that hour probably a better man than ever before.

Then come the weeks and months and years of soldiering far removed from home and restraining moral force- For many weary months—as in the Sinai Campaign—there is never the sight of a woman's face, never a softening or uplifting influence. Is it to be wondered that men grow coarse, that their manners and their language deteriorate? Almost the only relaxation they find is in gambling. Home folks will never believe to what an extent the gambling craze has captured the army in Egypt. It has been said that the first thing the Australians did in the Holy Land was to start a 'Two-up School'. Old hands on the transports and hospital ships make hundreds of pounds at the expense of soldiers coming to and from the war. Bookmakers and others at Tel el Kebir made thousands of pounds at 'Crown and Anchor' and 'Two-up' and other games out of the Australian soldiers.

Many of these spielers boasted of the amounts they had

cabled home to Australia to supplement their banking accounts Every pay-day in Palestine or Sinai or Egypt every camp was the signal for 'Two-up Schools' to start working, and thoughtless youths time and again lost the money that should have kept them in little luxuries to vary the bully-beef diet. It would be interesting to compute how many thousands of pounds changed hands in this way in the A.I.F. "Stop it?" As well attempt to stop the flow of the Nile.

If a hundred soldiers taken at random were asked the question, "What effect has soldiering had on your character?" I think the majority would honestly say it had not improved them. They would probably claim a wider knowledge of countries and men and life generally, and a broader charity and forbearance for the actions and opinions and beliefs of others. But I fear they would acknowledge a loss of ideals once held sacred, a too generous toleration of evil, a want of sympathy with strict rules of conduct and duty, and a cynical indifference to religion. This, of course, is only a phase. It will pass. But it is right here that the spiritual side of the Y.M.C.A. activities have been most valuable. It has, against great odds, fought all along the line for clean living and clean thinking and clean speech, for noble ideals, and a maintenance of the standards which soldiering inevitably undermines. It is a helpful sign to see how readily the soldiers respond to the Y.M.C.A. appeal. Out in the front line the spiritual side of their nature became deadened; they sagged morally. And the measure in which the Y.M.C.A. combats this influence and inspires the soldiers with spiritual ideals is the measure of its success in this department of its work.

In his delightful story, *Barlasch of the Guard,* Henry Seton Merriman says that war leaves no man as it found him: it either hardens his heart or the reverse. I wonder what will be the final verdict with regard to the war's effect on the Cameliers. They have known the solitude of Sinai, the excitement of Egypt, the appeal of Palestine, and the lust of battle as probably no other troops have. If these distracting influences in the final phase leave them better men than when they were mere civilians, then the credit will be largely due to the Y.M.C.A.

So the Y.M.C.A. followed the army on into Palestine, to Jerusalem, and Jaffa, and the Jordan, as near the front line as they were allowed. When we were in the Wadi Ghuzzie there were a dozen Y.M.C.A. dugouts scattered along the line. Some were within a few hundred yards of the front-line trenches. Here the boys came to write their home letters and see the home papers. During the heat of summer, lime-juice was served out gratis by day. As the nights grew cold, hot cocoa was given to the men at night. One little dugout would give out as many as a thousand cups of cocoa in one night.

The Y.M.C.A. now runs the Jerusalem Hotel in Jaffa, a splendid up-to-date soldiers' club in Jerusalem, a fine swimming-bath in the Esbekiyeh Gardens in Cairo, and scores of other propositions all calculated to help the soldiers. I wish all those public-spirited, wealthy folk back home, who give so generously to the Y.M.C.A., could realise how grateful the boys are for all these good things. We know it all costs millions sterling, and we know somebodies are footing the bill. And we're grateful.

CHAPTER 25

Camel Races

"War is Hell."
So said the American General. Perhaps he is right.
Still, war is not *all* Hell. Some phases of war are quite the reverse. So in the dim and distant future, when the boys go marching home, they will tell tall travellers' tales of the strange cities they have seen, and in these peaceful times to be, the Cameliers will forgather and talk about the sports they held in Egypt and Sinai and Palestine.

Mange and sore backs and debility, and the other ills camel-flesh is heir to, were specially preordained by a beneficent Providence in order to periodically withdraw the Camel Brigade from active warfare, so as to enable the Cameliers to satisfy their lust for sport. Hence the Camel Brigade sports have become an institution. The first big meeting was held at El Arish in February 1917, what time the Hun airmen proved themselves the only decent sports in the whole German army by paying a friendly visit. The second combined sports were held at Rafa in September the same year, when the Pennant was first made a bone of contention, and was carried off in triumph by the 2nd Battalion. Other minor gatherings have been staged by isolated companies at Assiut and Kubri, while the Reds retained pleasant recollections of the Ismailian sports, attended and witnessed by a galaxy of youthful beauty from that famous seaside resort.

With such a sporting record emblazoned on their A.F.B. 122 it was only to be expected that the Camel Brigade, having fixed up such minor details as the capture of Jerusalem and Jaffa and Beersheba and Gaza, should in the spring let its fancy lightly turn to thoughts of sport. A date was fixed. But Jupiter Pluvius proved unkind. It rained for fourteen days and fourteen nights. Then the Medical Officer, instead of concentrating his attention on fleas, accidentally held a sick parade and banished a couple of companies to the wilderness. However, all obstacles were eventually surmounted, and in the fullness of time—to wit, February 1918—the Third Great Sports Meeting of the Camel Brigade eventuated, and, lest we forget to mention it later on—was an unqualified success.

If this prosaic record of events were compiled for circulation amongst the uninitiated, it would have to suffer numberless explanatory interpolations. For the stranger cannot understand the wiles of the camel or the woes of the Camelier. For instance, should a stranger or a soldier chance to scan these lines he might ask why 'Kabrit', *alias* 'Mange Dressing', *alias* 'Onward', *alias* 'The Galoot', *alias* 'Murphy', could only scramble home a bad second in his heat in the camel trot, yet could show a clean pair of heels to the whole field in the final. Macaulay's schoolboy knows who won the Melbourne Cup, and why Bill Adams won the Battle of Waterloo, but even a University degree is useless when picking the winner of a camel scurry. So outsiders will not appreciate the situation, and since the Cameliers all know what happened, this serves merely to refresh their memory, and to remind their children what Daddy did in the Great War.

Well, the 1st Battalion won the pennant, won it handsomely, and, in the threatening language of the chief of the Red Flashes, they will fight mighty hard before they will release their grip of it. They fought hard for it, and well deserved their victory. But every dog must have his day, and as the

Black Pyramids handed over the symbol of their former glory, the Blues with one accord cried, "Our turn next!" The final points which decided the fate of the Pennant Championship for the ensuing period were:

1st Battalion	23½ points
4th Battalion	13½ points
2nd Battalion	11 points

There must always be one battalion minding the shop and cooee-ing as the steamers pass, homeward bound, through the Suez Canal, so the gallant 'Thirds' were missing from the tourney. Still, they were well represented by their burly quartermaster, who assisted in the judging, and went back home fairly bristling with points for the edification of the Green Triangles.

Let not the judges, stewards, and committee say that theirs was a thankless task, for they are hereby thanked heartily and gratefully by the whole brigade for the unselfish labours which made the sports such a pronounced success. It was invidious to particularise: from the time the Engineers started laying out the ground till the man with the megaphone yelled "Out!" all went well; and anyhow virtue is its own reward. Alas for poor old Newson! He was clerk of the course, and his cry of "Out!" as each successive competitor failed to clear the high jump quite tickled the crowd. Yet within a few weeks he himself was out, killed by a treacherous foe at Amman, after the Turks had surrendered.

One would like to place on record some appreciation of the splendid enthusiasm and painstaking efforts which were concentrated on the best turned-out section. Practically all the competitors were turned out fit for a King's Review. The ensemble, as the sections were lined up prior to judging, was brilliant. Right gladly will C.O.'s fork out the 'feluce' (from regimental funds) for Kiwi and Blanco and paint and polish.

Once again the 2nd Battalion proved pre-eminent in this department. Seven and Nine being bracketed top, with Seventeen and One fighting for second place, and Four next in order of merit.

The tables were turned in the next event, for the Reds secured the first five places in the midday halt—the 1st Battalion H.Q. leading the four companies home.

The fickle goddess Fortune having first favoured the Seconds and Firsts, now smiled on the Fourths. The wrestling on camels now proved a most popular event, stubbornly contested. The 'Eighteens', with Avard in the van, finally managed to unhorse Hamilton's bunch, leaving number Nine to fill third place. In the Indian section some strenuous scuffling resulted in 'B' section of the Bing Boys downing the 'A's.' In the gun competition also the same section carried off the honours, mounting their gun and dismounting with commendable celerity.

Considerable interest centred in the high jump, but on account of the sandy nature of the ground no records were broken. Fielder dually won home, with Newman next in the list, and the Indian Singh quartet some distance back. Pretty much the same field assembled for the hop, step, and jump, which Footner won with 36 feet 5½ inches, next in order being Stevens, 36 feet 4 inches, and Dunstan 35 feet 7½ inches.

With Sully and Cochrane out of the hunt, it was hard to pick the winner of the 100-yards championship. The heat winners were Shaha Khan, Bayley, M'Namara, with Hamilton and Ash running a dead heat in the last prelim. The final, however, went to Footner, who had been beaten by Bayley in the second heat. Second and third places were filled by M'Namara and Shaha Khan. This event showed the battalions how to pick their relay teams, and an exciting run followed. A dropped flag at a critical moment blighted many hopes. Eventually the Blues scored a splendid win, with Reds second, and the Field Ambulance third.

The outside world—lacking the advantages enjoyed by the

Cameliers—has no idea how fast a camel can trot or gallop. For the first few times one sees a camel galloping nothing is more ludicrous and mirth-provoking. But much water has passed under the bridge at El Arish since first we saw camels fully extended. So we just forgot how funny it used to look, and focused our attention on their pace. The trot was run in four heats and a final, the finalists being 'The Quack' and 'Kabrit', 'Jamestown' and 'John Lobban', 'Starlight' and 'Scotch Mist', 'Strychnine' and 'Cyanide'. Most fancied were 'Strychnine', 'Starlight', 'Kabrit', and 'The Quack'. The last named had beaten 'Kabrit' in the first heat, but in a subsequent try-out 'Kabrit' had shown such a clean pair of heels to 'The Quack' that the latter fell from grace. 'Strychnine' was known to be very fast, but very erratic on the post. So followers of form sent the camels to the post with 'Kabrit' and 'Starlight' favourites. Their judgement was vindicated, for amid intense excitement and the hilarious yells of successful punters, 'Kabrit' cantered home a length ahead of 'Cyanide', with 'Starlight' third.

There were several 'Unknowns' in the camel scurry, and possibly some 'dark horses'. However, the cognoscenti of the Reds, remembering how 'Horace' had mopped up the opposition down on the Canal, stuck to their favourite. 'Bedouin Chief', 'Joe', 'Gaza', and 'Tom Thumb' were also in request. The preliminary heats sent the following to the post for the final: 'Horace' and 'Tom Thumb', 'Bedouin Chief' and 'Sappy', 'Francis' and 'Poppy', 'Bluey' and 'Gaza'. The field got away to a good start, and old 'Horace' at once showed prominently. He galloped like a champion and never looked like being beaten, finally passing the post over a length ahead of 'Tom Thumb', 'Gaza' coming with a rush into third position.

As a mirth-provoker the egg and spoon race on camels was *some* stunt. Maybe it was the pained expression on the face of the riders, or perhaps the supercilious indifference of the camels. Anyhow, the crowd yelled with delight. The winner turned up in Sergeant Floyd, with Rur Singh second.

No less diverting was the musical chairs. Here again the camels hardly entered into the spirit of the chase. If camels *do* think, then they must wonder why Allah ever permitted these Cameliers to cross the seas and make merry at the expense, of the erstwhile dignified dromedaries. From the medley of shouts and music and halters and camels and sand-bags, Hargreaves captured the prize, with Connors and Foyle also securing a few piastres, and thirty others in the 'also ran' department.

In the bayonet fighting Competition some excellent teams lost many points through not appearing in full marching order. The prize went to No. 2 Company, with No. 9 second, and the Machine Gunners third. Considerable interest centred in the section area bivouac, though the suggestion that the keenness of the contestants was due to the prize being a barrel of beer is staunchly repudiated. After carefully considering the pros and cons, the judges decided for Nos. 10, 17, and 3. If the thirst of the competitors had been taken into consideration, the result would have been far different.

From the time the idea of holding a sports meeting was first mooted, the hefty men of the Reds, Blues, and Blacks have been asking themselves the question, "Can we beat the Bing Boys in the tug-of-war?" The Indians thought not. However, the battalions had a very hard try to down the gunners, but failed. The final between the Blues and the Battery was witnessed by a great crowd of cheering spectators. It was a strenuous tussle, but resulted, as all previous similar contests, in victory for the Hong-Kong and Singapore Battery. The battalions have the requisite strength for the job; next time it is hoped they will settle down and train their teams solidly, and then in all probability—the Bing Boys will win again.

There was much speculation over the horse events, and considerable uncertainty. Several days before the race, fancy prices were taken about some of the hacks. In the Arab section there was a division of opinion which was settled, to the surprise of some, by 'Bint' romping home ahead of 'Mahamidiya' and

'O'Bee'. For the others, Class 1., 'Asquith', was mostly favoured, with 'Touch and Go', 'First In', 'Blue Spec', and 'Chester' in some demand. Long odds had been given about 'Buster Brown', and a well-informed clique of Red Flashes risked good piastres on him. Had 'Asquith' been more tractable he might have landed the prize, but just when the crowd began to yell, "Asquith, Asquith!" the Doc cried, "Wait and see!" and Holland came with a fine rush and got 'Buster Brown' first past the box.

Naturally the main witticism over the Class 2. event was to the effect that 'Fleas' had been scratched. But this was only a rumour. Lieut. Holland carried off the double by steering Dr. de Boer's 'Fleas' to the front, to the surprise of almost everybody.

A big field faced the starter for the 'All Comers' Officers' Pony Race, but despite the stable rumours anent the invincibility of 'Ginger', Major Buxton's 'Mahogany' streaked home an easy winner. There were two concerts in the evening to top off the day's sport.

As a wind-up to the meeting, the G.O.C., Brigadier-General C. L. Smith, V.C., M.C., presented the prizes to the successful competitors, and congratulated them all on their prowess. The pennant, with cheers, was handed to Lieut.-Colonel G. F. Langley, and now flutters proudly in the breeze before the wigwam of the chief of the Red Flashes. It will probably be presented to the Australian War Museum.

The victory of the many-named 'Kabrit' in the Camel Cup was celebrated in the following lines:

> What's in a name?
> *There was a gallant Camelier, whose name was Patsy Murphy,*
> *And every time he told a tale, the boys said, "It's a furphy."*
> *Now, Murphy found a camel, and he thought it was a trier;*
> *But when he tried its paces, sure, it proved to be a flier.*
> *So he christened it with whisky, and he called it 'The Galoot',*
> *And entered it to win the Camel Cup down at Assiut.*
> *The boys were in no hurry*

To back it for the scurry,
But Murphy didn't worry, for Murphy bagged the loot.

The Camel Corps swung eastward to the wilds of El Arish,
But Murphy, sure, was stony broke—all his felouce mafish.
So when the sports came round again, Pat Murphy saw his chance,
He called his camel 'Onward', and he led the books a dance;
They'd never heard of 'Onward', so they gave him ten to one.
But Murphy had them thinking, at the setting of the sun.
For 'Onward' proved a winner,
For the books it was a skinner;
Pat had whisky with his dinner, sure, the world was made for fun.

In course of time the 'Fighting First' went down to Ferry Post;
The boys all started training with the hacks they fancied most,
But to the sports a camel came which set the old hands guessing,
They seemed to know the animal, but not the name
   'Mange Dressing'.
But Murphy wasn't far away, he risked his last piastre,
And still the camel stood to him and saved him from disaster.
It was just as he intended,
For when the day was ended,
Some camels were just splendid, but 'Mange Dressing'
   travelled faster.

Now, every dog must have his day, but Murphy's day lasts years,
He seems to have the luck of half a dozen Cameliers;
For when the I.C.C. camped in the Land of Milk and Honey,
Pat Murphy and his camel won another pot of money.
We all had speedy camels that we fancied for the trot;
'The Quack' was fast, 'Starlight' was fine, and 'Strychnine'
   was red-hot.
But Murphy made a hit,
With his mount—now called 'Kabrit',
For the wretch was simply it; it's time the brute was shot.

CHAPTER 26

The Soldier

There is a well-known and stirring battle poem beloved of the Irish, which, quoting from memory, begins like this:

*Thrice at the heights of Fontenoy the English column failed,
And twice the lines of St. Antoine the Dutch in vain assailed.*

This couplet has been parodied for the benefit of the Turkish communiqué, which claims:

*Thrice at the heights of Amman the English column failed,
And twice the Hedjaz Railway, Anzacs in vain assailed.*

However, the Turkish communiqué is not absolutely correct. Thrice indeed the right wing of Allenby's army crossed the Jordan and moved up through the mountains towards the railway. On the first occasion a flying column of Light Horse and Cameliers, supported by London infantry, was sent out to capture Es Salt, threaten Amman, and blow up the Hedjaz Railway. All this was accomplished, yet, as shall be explained, the venture was not an absolute success. The second stunt was purely a demonstration, a kind of Jeb Stewart cavalry dash, for the Anzacs had express orders not to go beyond Es Salt, not even to enter that town, for fear the Turks would make reprisals on any of the Christians there who welcomed the British. This stunt was quite successful. The third venture was rather unlucky. Shunet Nimrin—captured in the first stunt and abandoned—happened to have a double garrison, for the Turks were changing over when the British attacked. However, the splendid work of the Anzacs in the mountains, and the capture of several hundred Turks and Germans, more than neutralised this set-back. The loss of nine guns is admittedly one to Abdul.

The Cameliers participated in the first venture only. So I leave to other and abler chroniclers the task of telling how splendidly the New Zealand Mounted Rifles and the Australian Light Horse and the London Tommies fought in the subsequent frays into the land of Gilead.

When the Turks retired north and east after the capture of Jericho, they blew to smithereens the concrete bridge over the Jordan at Ghoraniyeh. It thus became necessary to secure new crossings and establish bridgeheads before, the army could move over preparatory to advancing against Amman. Perhaps some of the Anzac engineers will tell how, in face of snipers and machine guns and big guns and a raging torrent, they swam the Jordan, threw ropes across, then made a pontoon-bridge, and finally established a safe bridgehead. Anyhow, when the Camel Brigade reached the Makhadet Ford, just north of the Dead Sea, the engineers—what was left of them—were sitting down and smoking contentedly. So, with some persuasion, the camels crossed the swaying pontoons, fearful of the yellow current surging below, and we moved out over the Jordan, even as did the two and a half tribes of the Children of Israel many years before.

On 22nd March the crossing was forced, and the Anzacs, spreading fan-wise, east and northwards, cleared out the Turks on the eastern bank; after them came the London infantry, Camel Brigade, artillery, Field Ambulances, demolition parties, and supplies. Shunet Nimrin had first to be captured, as it barred the main road up to Es Salt and Amman. So with splendid gallantry the Cockneys advanced to the assault. Behind them the artillery thundered, while the Anzac Mounted

Division swung wide on the flanks, threatening the rear. Kabr Mujahid was occupied, and the road from Madeba blocked on the south. On the north the Mounteds pushed on *via* the Wadi Meidan road. The position of Nimrin was now precarious, and the garrison, fearful for their rear, soon succumbed to the attacking Londoners.

Three roads now lay invitingly before the British, and along these the army pushed towards Amman. Then the weather—which had been fine—swung round all in favour of Abdul. It rained day after day. The rough mountain tracks became almost impassable. The Walers ploughed through. Infantry struggled on up to their knees in mud, frequently fording wadis in spate three feet deep. Camels slithered and slid all over the place. Pack animals laden with explosives gave their drivers hair-raising thrills every minute. The Cameliers dismounted and led their mounts all the night—a night they will long remember. It is on record that one patch of mountain track was so precarious that in twelve hours the column covered less than 200 yards. Now and then a pack camel, top-heavy with explosives or ammunition, would lose its footing and topple over a precipice. Once a beast slipped and fell over the cliff, turned numerous somersaults, then to the surprise of all landed on its feet and started grazing contentedly. Then on they went in the mud, mud, mud.

In due—or overdue—course the Flying Column reached their objective. The Anzacs, with impetuous dash, charged at Es Salt, and captured the garrison amid the plaudits and thanks of the populace. Then they swept on to Amman. But the German 'planes flying over the Plains of Jericho had seen the league-long columns of horse, foot, camelry, and artillery crossing the Jordan. Reinforcements were hurriedly entrained and sent down from Damascus. If the rain had held off another day or two, all would have gone swimmingly; but the Turkish reinforcements reached Amman in time to be thrown into the firing line. Our information was that the town was garrisoned only by a few hundreds. But when our attack developed Abdul had several thousands to oppose us, and more on the way. The demolition project was, however, persisted in. The Cameliers swung round on to the Hedjaz Railway, blew up Kissir Station, some culverts, and five miles of the permanent way. The Light Horse brushed aside all opposition, and, reaching the line, blew up the main arches of the railway bridge over the wadi. Unfortunately the damage done here was not beyond repair. But the stiff defence put up opposite Amman itself prevented the blowing up of the railway tunnel.

Opposed to the strong force of Turks now in Amman the Flying Column only had two companies of London Irish and a portion of the Camel Brigade, with Light Horse and New Zealand Mounted Rifles, and the Bing Boys' battery of mountain guns operating on either flank. The Turks, with a dozen guns skilfully concealed, were posted on a commanding eminence, Hill 3039, and this had to be taken. At three in the morning, in the midst of a cold, misty rain, the Cameliers—English, Scotties, and Anzacs—attacked. Creeping up under cover of darkness, they were upon the Turkish trenches before the alarm could be given. Then with a wild yell the Cameliers threw themselves upon the dazed defenders. There was fierce bayonet work, scores of Turks were killed, and the remainder threw up their hands. The first line having surrendered, the Cameliers pushed on to the second trench. But this left unguarded a number of Turks and Germans in the front fine who had yelled for quarter. With Teutonic treachery several of these grabbed the rifles they had thrown down and fired on the backs of the men who had spared their lives. In this way was Lieut. Newson killed, one of the most popular officers in the Camel Brigade. Some of the Cameliers, with 'Matt' in the van, charged right on till they reached Amman itself. But their ranks had been thinned, and Turkish reinforcements were still coming up. So they retired to the hill, dug in, and awaited developments. Then came the getaway.

CHAPTER 27

The Soldier

The Indians working the Camel battery of mountain guns did splendid execution till their ammunition gave out. They swore and tore their hair, as excellent targets presented themselves and not a shell left. The O.C., however, managed to borrow a few rounds from a British battery which came up, and they resumed their work. But the German guns behind the town knew the range to a nicety, and did considerable execution among our ranks. The firing line—New Zealanders, Irish, Scots, English, Indians, and Australians—hung on to the ground they had gained till the demolition parties had finished their job. Then word came for the retirement.

Several hundred prisoners and much munitions had already been sent back to Ghoraniyeh, and the task of evacuating the wounded was proceeding apace. Now if Abdul had been really alive to the situation he might have so harried and hurried our retreat as to make it a ticklish business; but he evidently had not the slightest idea of our movements. Anticipating another attack, he was feverishly improving his defences, what time our infantry and artillery were quietly tripping back to the Jordan. Without a hitch the army meandered along the mountain tracks in long, snake-like columns, leaving the Anzac Light Horse and the Cameliers to bring up the rear.

For a day or two the Hun 'planes swarmed over Jericho and the Jordan and Shunet Nimrin, reconnoitring our movements, and at times their bombing squadrons heavily bombed our lines. The exact damage done need not be mentioned here, but—as illustrating the luck of the game—it may be told that one bomb landed fair in a bivvy occupied by four officers. Two were killed outright, the one next them escaped scathless, the fourth had his leg blown off.

So in due course the Flying Column returned to the Plains of Jericho. Our casualties, considering the nature of the expedition, were not numerous. The enemy, in killed, wounded, and prisoners, lost far more heavily. But the Cameliers mourn the loss of Saunderson from Westralia, Newson from England, Adolf, the brilliant footballer, from New Zealand, and several more officers and men who a week before had so light-heartedly crossed the ancient river.

Then it suddenly dawned on Jacko that the army which had the temerity to push so far into his territory had quietly melted away. All unmolested now, the Turk came along the same mountain roads, expecting an ambush at every boulder. Reaching the foot-hills he was finally convinced of the getaway. So he gathered his forces, and on 11th April made a very determined onslaught on our bridgehead at Ghoraniyeh. But Fighting Charlie Cox's Light Horsemen, with some London infantry and machine gunners, had been just itching for Jacko to do this very thing. They lay doggo till the Turks had definitely committed themselves to the attack. Then our artillery blazed away at known ranges and plumped unceasing salvos of shrapnel on the crowded ranks of the enemy. Machine guns in carefully chosen possies opened a devastating fusillade, while the infantry amongst the scrub added their quota. As Cromwell would have said, "The Lord had delivered them into our hands." As the careless Anzacs put it, "It was a shame to take the money." The Turks halted and wavered and then turned in full retreat. This was the signal for the Light Horsemen, who raced their horses out of the wadi tributaries, and charged the fleeing foe.

In the attack on Nimrin and Amman the Turks, besides killed and wounded, lost over 700 prisoners and 4 pieces of artillery. In this abortive counter-attack they had nearly 400 killed alone, many wounded, and nearly 100 prisoners, while our casualties were insignificant. So said the official communiqué. But for every lone grave on the Jordan side or on Amman Ridge there's a broken-hearted woman way back in Australia.

As Brentomnan puts it:

There's a church bell rings down the Hawkesbury
When the night hush hovers near;
And an old boat swings on the Hawkesbury,
Longside an old worn pier.
There's an old wife dreams o'er the Hawkesbury,
By the pier and the swaying spar,
While prayer-ships swim out o'er the Hawkesbury.
To seas and strange lands afar.

There's an old camp down by the Jordan-side,
And an old bloke a-weary there
For a mate gone over the Jordan-side,
And a bivvy-sheet to spare;
For a task that films all the Jordan-side
In a mistiness of tears,
And a tale far-flung from the Jordan-side
To the Hawkesbury's listening ears.

There's a new-made grave on the Amman Ridge,
Where no limelights staked a claim,
Though some brave blood crimsoned the Amman Ridge
With the 'red' that knows the game.
But the Hawkesbury to the Amman Ridge
Is a forlorn cry and wide,
And the Bedouin prowls o'er the Amman Ridge
With the dead that the mountains hide.

An incident not unworthy of note was the exodus of Christians and others from Es Salt and the neighbourhood when our troops entered. These seized the opportunity to flee to Jericho and on to Judaea, and so place themselves under the protection of the British flag. Many leading citizens of Es Salt welcomed joyfully the advent of the British, but when they found it was only a raid on a big scale, with a return to the Jordan in a few days, they knew the Turks would deal harshly with them for their manifestation of sympathy with Britain. So they too packed up their treasures and bolted to Jericho. One disappointed citizen speaking excellent English remarked, "It took the English four years to get to Es Salt. It took them only four days to get away."

There are few things more pitiful than a people fleeing from their homes in the face of an army. Here, however, the exodus was accompanied by none of those heart-rending scenes which marked the Serbian debacle. These were mostly well-to-do people. Scores of them had horses and donkeys. Many of them, however, had just taken up their beds and walked. Long lines of refugees, carrying huge bundles on their backs, trudged steadily westward to the Jordan and on to Jericho.

Soon the ancient city was filled to overflowing. In the streets and gardens and houses were thousands of homeless, mostly women and children and old men.

The quixotic chivalry of some Cameliers was exemplified by an incident at Mujahid. A party of Bedouins, heavily laden, was making for the Jordan. But while seven or eight women of assorted ages were carrying huge bundles, about a dozen men were striding along unhampered. So the Cameliers stopped the procession, and made the poor old women drop their bundles. Several of the heftiest young men were selected, and ordered to pick up the impedimenta. But this was contrary to all their traditions. It was a unique experience. They demurred. But the Australians sent the women on ahead, and gently applied the boot till the astounded males grasped the situation—and the bundles. Amid derisive cheers of the Cameliers the party moved off, the scowling Bedouins labouring under the unaccustomed, burdens. . . .

Of course when they had gone on a mile or so and were out of range of the interfering Cameliers, they promptly dropped their loads, the women resumed their proper role in the Bedouin business, and became beasts of burden again.

Chapter 28

Kantara

Kantara has changed. In the old days, before Romani, it was a dreary caravanserai. It is now a delight to pass through Kantara. Light Horsemen and Cameliers coming in from the never-never country in Sinai find in Kantara a refreshing oasis.

The reason for this? Simply that two Australian ladies came to Kantara. Now there are thousands of Australian ladies doing splendid war work back home, or in England, or France, or Egypt. But when the Light Horsemen start heaving bouquets about, they think first of these two ladies at Kantara. Tired troopers trekking to town, sick of the scorching sands of Sinai, find their first full feed at Kantara. Dirty and travel-stained, with a week's whiskers on their sunburnt faces, they find rest and comfort and a cheery Australian welcome. There are flowers (real flowers), butter (real butter, on ice), fruit salad, and nice soft fresh bread. It's just like a breath of Australia.

Kantara is "the bridge" joining Asia and Africa. It is on the old caravan route from the East. For thousands of years the shambling camel trains from Palestine have passed through here and on to Cairo. Then, when war awakened Sinai to life and activity, Kantara began to assume the importance and dimensions of a port. The army of Egypt marched through. Then came the rebound. Sick and wounded soldiers came back through Kantara to the Cairo hospitals. When the scrapping eased up, men came through on leave. But they had to sleep on the Canal side. There was nothing to eat except the bully beef they brought with them. Men were only too glad to shake the dust of Kantara off their feet, and train for Cairo.

The need for some half-way house was early felt. Many folk thought of it, and many more spoke of it. Then on Anniversary Day, 26th January 1917, the Soldiers' Rest was opened by Mrs. William Chisholm and Miss Rainey M'Phillamy. There was one little marquee, one small spirit stove, one mule, one water-cart, one big table—quite a modest beginning, was it not? Yet already over 250,000 men have passed through. As many as 4000 soldiers have been fed and cheered in a single day, and 5000 eggs have been sacrificed between dawn and midnight. The Soldiers' Home has increased and prospered. There are now several big tents and a substantial hut. There are huge ovens and ice-chests, and bread bins and cake baskets and boilers, and about twenty-five big tables. The original staff of two has increased until now there are 30 assistants—all 'B' class men from Moascar.

Though the two cheerful pioneers do not mention it, one can readily guess at the strenuous times they had in the beginning. Trains arrived at all hours, and soldiers sauntered into the canteen for a snack. The 'Open all night' notice was not up, but men came along just the same. Sometimes for two or three days on end the ladies never had a chance to get to bed. A couple of times the tent was blown down, and dust storms made life miserable. Then came torrential rains. There were millions of mosquitoes. Water was scarce. Eggs went bad. A rush of hungry soldiers time and again cleared out the larder. But the indefatigable workers just smiled and carried on.

All the officials on the line of communication were most kind. But officialdom was as usual fairly apathetic. Miles of red tape had to be cut through. A rest hut, something more substantial than a tent, was urgently required, and there were scores and scores of empty huts laying idle at Tel el Kebir and other deserted camps. But no one would give the ladies the necessary timber. So £150 had to be paid for a little bit of timber for a hut. Wood is very dear in Egypt. Tanks were needed badly. All recognised how much they were required; but no one could give or sell them. So a couple of enterprising young Australians just sauntered off and 'found' a couple of empty tanks.

The main object of the canteen is to give a rest and a welcome and a cheap meal to all soldiers passing through Kantara. It is not confined to Australians. The men get the same food as the officers, only the men pay seven piastres and the officers ten. All the profits go back to the boys in the shape of more food and luxuries, and better accommodation. On one occasion word came that a whole division of Territorials was to detrain at Kantara. Mrs. Chisholm promptly wired to Cairo and Port Said for a huge stock of bread, cakes, eggs, and fruit, and the Tommies had a glorious and most unexpected feast.

Another time a perspiring orderly rushed in to say that 80 officers would be in to lunch, and could they be accommodated? The ladies smiled and said "Yes." Five minutes later another excited Tommy bolted in to say that the officers would not be in to lunch. The ladies sat down and breathed a sigh of relief. Three minutes after the 80 officers arrived. An hour later they went away well fed and happy, wondering withal why the army could not feed them as satisfactorily and graciously as these Australian ladies.

Many an Australian mother, could she see this Kantara canteen at night, would bless the motherly care of Mrs. Chisholm; and many a trooper, returning to the dangers and privations of the desert campaign, thinks gratefully of the smiling greeting and kindly welcome of the little Australian girl at Kantara. At first officialdom was sceptical, then tolerant, then relieved, and finally enthusiastic. Nowadays when the boys are sent in from Palestine to a school at Zietoun or a rest camp at Port Said, arrangements are made for them to breakfast at Mrs. Chisholm's. And going back to the firing fine, they write home paying generous tribute, to the Kantara canteen. In the fullness of time this chorus of praise reached the ears of the powers that be, and the whole A.I.F. was delighted beyond measure when the official announcement was made that Mrs. Chisholm and Miss M'Phillamy had been decorated with the Order of the British Empire.

Time came when the theatre of war was shifted from Sinai to Palestine. The army moved on beyond Jerusalem and over the Jordan. And always there were men coming and going. Some were on duty, some sick, some on leave. And they all had to wait an hour or a day or a night at Jerusalem. But there was no accommodation for them. The need for a rest camp at Jerusalem was as badly felt as had been the need for one at Kantara.

So Miss M'Phillamy got busy. Once again there was the initial trouble with rules and regulations, but several Generals, knowing the good work done at Kantara, put their influence into the scale. All the officers concerned were courteous and sympathetic. Only officialdom was apathetic. But in course of time the Empire Soldiers' Club was established on the outskirts of the Holy City. Miss M'Phillamy soon had everything running smoothly, and all the boys coming up from the Jordan side found a home from home and a cheery welcome. There were troubles and worries at first on account of the lack of accommodation. A dignified senior supply officer was nonplussed one hot morning when an orderly handed him an urgent message from the young lady in charge of the Soldiers' Club. It ran: "I have half a bullock and a ton of onions in my bedroom. *Please* send wood for a storeroom."

CHAPTER 29

The Soldier

This is the story of Musellabeh—at least one little chapter of its eventful history, for Musellabeh is as old as the ages. When the trumpets of the Israelites sounded round ancient Jericho, Musellabeh heard the clarion note echoing and re-echoing from the hills. But of its previous record the Cameliers knew nothing and cared less.

Up on the heights of Bethlehem spring had only just awakened the wild flowers to beauty. Hill and dale were clothed in a carpet of splendour. The wadis were ablaze with scarlet poppies. The wind that played over the Judæan hills was cool and bracing, and at night it was cold enough to make the Cameliers snuggle close under their three or four blankets.

Then, skirting the walls of Jerusalem, we went by Bethany into Jericho. And down by the Dead Sea it seemed that we had dropped from winter into the cauldron of midsummer. And down in the valley by the ford where John the Baptist preached and baptised, the Camel Brigade crossed the Jordan and, climbing the Anti-Lebanon range, smote the men of Amman, hip and thigh.

Coming back from their adventure—the Turkish communique called it a misadventure—in the land of Gilead, the Camel Brigade left their mounts grazing contentedly on the Plains of Jericho—not too contentedly, for the Hun 'planes bombed the area repeatedly, and did some damage now and then. On foot we therefore went forward and took over the line, stretching from the Jordan to the mountains. And there we stayed for some weeks while the summer sun scorched and blistered our faces, while enemy artillery splattered shrapnel over our lines, while flies by the million made day a misery, while venomous mosquitoes at night made us forget all about the flies, and while snakes and scorpions at all hours reminded us that there are worse things than war.

Where the foot-hills settle down on to the plain, Musellabeh rises imposingly up, the last protest of the disappearing mountains against the levelling hand of time. It was the strongest point in our line—probably that was why Jacko was so anxious to secure it. Anyhow, he made half a dozen attacks before he was finally convinced that the game was not worth the candle. He had made a few abortive attempts while the British infantry held the hill, but when the Cameliers came along early in April, the Huns reckoned it was high time the position was captured. They began—on 8th April—by subjecting the old hill to a furious bombardment. To be sure, Jacko was, during the whole month, most lavish with his shells. And because the hill was mostly rock and our fire possies were rather shallow, we had a few casualties.

Some glimpse at the topography of the place is necessary to appreciate the situation. Our trenches on the hill faced north. Running north past our right flank and on to Damascus was the old Romani Road. Right in front of the hill was a deep ravine, and from this rose the steep sides of a hill, half a mile long, known as Green Hill. Farther north and a little bit west was Brown Hill, or Beghalet. To westward rose the mountains like bastions, and here the enemy guns were nicely hidden, while their observation officers could see a man if he so much as moved a yard from his funk-hole on Musellabeh. From the mountains a dozen shallow wadis meandered towards the three hills, giving excellent opportunities for Jacko to sneak up and congregate in the ravine between Musellabeh and Green Hill. Away east, the plain gently subsided into the Wadi Mellahah and the river Jordan.

So it was over Green Hill and the little wadis that the Turks first advanced to the attack, about a battalion strong. But the British artillery was posted in likely spots some distance behind Musellabeh, and when the first wave of the attack, about 200 strong, moved forward, our barrage swooped down and cut them off from the supports, who remained impotent behind Green Hill. Coming on, the Turks came under a well-directed rifle fire from our trenches, to which their response was feeble and ineffective. Then our barrage, shortening, poured shrapnel on to them and took all the sting out of their attack. The German guns meanwhile made excellent practice, landing salvos all along the hill in advance of the attack. Eventually the move was brought to a standstill, with the Turks in the ravine and under the brow of Musellabeh. Our guns continued to play on them, and when darkness shielded them from observation they slunk back over Green Hill, whence they came. When next Jacko advanced, he surely never meant to take the place. His raiders managed to effect a lodgement in our unoccupied possies low on the north-east corner of the hill. From this spot they were summarily ejected. For their venture they showed nothing but their casualties.

A subsequent demonstration, productive of no result whatever, preceded their main attack on 11th April. A violent bombardment at dawn presaged the coming storm, and after a reckless expenditure of shrapnel and high explosives they came on. German officers and non-commissioned officers urged on the attackers, while German machine gunners, from vantage posts on Green Hill, concentrated a fusillade on our trenches. Under cover of this barrage the enemy managed to negotiate Green Hill without much opposition, and got into the ravine. The telephone wires connecting our front line with our artillery were severed by the hail of shells, so our guns were silent. All unmolested, Jacko prepared for the final assault. A company crept up the steep front of the hill, while a couple of platoons swung westward and enveloped our left wing. Here also, they enjoyed the shelter of the hillside, and were able to heave grenades, effectually attacking our left rear. M'Kenzie's section was then taken from the centre of the line to block this threatening move, and then for an hour or two there ensued a bombing duel. At first our bombs fell harmlessly over the Turks' heads, till the bombers lobbed them gently on the brow of the hill and the momentum caused them to roll nicely on Jacko ere they exploded.

Meanwhile the frontal attack developed. The Turks crept up the hill, but just as they were in position to fire at our centre they came under well-directed rifle and machine-gun fire from our right. This checked the onslaught, so the affair resolved itself into a battle of grenades at close range, each side for the most part being but of sight of the other; but our thin line of Anzacs had only a limited supply of bombs, and in places these gave out, so for luck the defenders heaved big boulders over the brow of the hill on to the hidden enemy.

There were some splendid deeds of derring-do performed on Musellabeh that day. Signallers ran out and joined up the wire under a heavy hail of shrapnel. From battalion headquarters the 'soft job' men staggered laden with bombs, which, under heavy fire, they carried to the front line. Orderlies time and again ran the gauntlet carrying orders and messages to and from the firing line. Dozens of men were wounded and several were killed. Reinforcements were hurried up from the supports, and the sorely tried front line had a well-earned respite. But for hours Jacko hung round the base of Musellabeh and in the ravine. Rifle grenades let him see that we were still ready for the 'Call of Stoush', but in dribs and drabs, risking the rifle fire from the hill, he melted away, leaving the Cameliers undisputed masters of Musellabeh.

A never-failing theme for discussion is the luck of the game. Old originals of Gallipoli and Romani and Gaza were killed on this ancient hill. During the day one solitary shell landed in the spot where battalion headquarters were camped, and it killed young Signaller W. E. Smith, who had run the gauntlet of the hill a dozen times, and had a score of times escaped death by a hairbreadth, only to meet his fate in a dugout far from the firing line. Lieut. A. R. Nield, known and loved as 'Ranji' by the whole Camel Corps, was killed, and every other officer on the hill at the time was wounded.

When the relief came in, we dug in deeper. At night the lads we lost were buried, the casualties were hurried off, and the old 'Doc' worked overtime. Next morning we again awaited the onslaught, but Jacko sulked behind Brown Hill, and let his artillery vent its wrath on Musellabeh. Then for a week Abdul hardly showed his face. An odd sniper or two let fly occasionally, and a few tired Turks were seen going to and from Brown Hill and Green Hill. Out on the plain their cavalry patrols moved hither and yon. And we dug and dug and dug, and wired our front, and linked up our line, till Musellabeh was like unto Achi Baba. Of course the enemy guns blazed away at all hours of the day and night. But we never worried much; Abdul had had enough. The only things we worried about were the snakes and scorpions and spiders and the mosquitoes. But by day the swarms of flies made us forget our other ills.

Anon General Allenby came along and congratulated the Cameliers on their performance. Captain Mills, who was in command of the hill during the main attack, got a bar to his M.C., and Military Crosses were awarded to Lieuts. M'Kenzie and Holland. Several decorations were awarded to the rank and file, and the c.-in-c. proclaimed in orders that to commemorate the defence, Musellabeh would in future be known as "The Camel's Hump".

The following verses essay to portray the stunt in more picturesque language than the above account:

The Camel's Hump

They called it Musellabeh in the days of long ago,
When old Joshua and the Israelites were there;
When caravans from East and West meandered to and fro,
And the war cry of the Hebrews filled the air.
It's a bold and rugged mountain, rising sheer above the plain
Like a camel to its belly bogged in mud;
And the hill was red with poppies in the Springtime after rain,
But today the hill is redder far—with blood.

Oh! the new crusading Anzacs crossed the Jordan's flowing tide,
And they smote the men of Amnion hip and thigh;
They cantered into Jericho, and took it in their stride,
And charged the Hun with murder in their eye.
Then the little English Tommies, trudging gamely through
   the heat,
Took the foot-hills of the Lebanon and stayed;
They camped on Musellabeh, with the Turk in full retreat,
And they shelled him—lest his going be delayed.

Oh! the Camel Corps swung northward with the Dead Sea
   far behind,
Left the camels grazing happy in the rear;
They took over Musellabeh, which the Tommies said was kind,
For it wasn't very healthy living there.
Then 'Jacko' came in thousands, Musellabeh to regain,
With his horsemen, footmen, airmen, and his guns.
And the battle raged with fury as he charged across the plain,
Food for slaughter, at the bidding of the Huns.

German gunners in the highlands loosed their wrath
   upon the hill,
The ground was rent and shattered with their shells;
And the thinning Camel phalanx yelled a fierce defiance till
Their dying groans were mingled with their yells.
They blazed away unceasing, gasping hard and gritting teeth,

They bombed till all their bombs had given out;
Then they heaved big mountain boulders on the enemy beneath,
And still retained their grip on the redoubt.

Oh! the British guns came roaring up the valley to the fight,
And their barrage fire caught 'Jacko' in the neck;
And the gunners toiled like Trojans all the day and half the night,
Till 'Abdul' quit, and handed in his check.
Then the Camels took a breather, and they gathered up the slain,
Tho' they wished that every Turk had been a Hun;
For they rather like old 'Jacko', and they hate to give him pain,
But war is war—and battles must be won.

Oh! Allenby came smiling o'er the hills of Palestine,
And victory came hot upon his track.
He sent congratulations to the Camels—said 'twas fine;
Said he knew that we could keep the blighters back.
And to celebrate the battle, lest the world forget the deed,
And the day we gave the foeman such a bump,
Now and henceforth and for ever, he solemnly decreed,
Musellabeh should be called "The Camel's Hump".

The report in the official communique, however, was much more concise. It was as follows:

"An attack on our right was repulsed with loss."

CHAPTER 30

Sister and Soldier

Summer swooped down with scorching wings on the valley of the Jordan. It was too hot to eat—let alone fight. So the armies marked time.

Now and then a gun loosed off apologetically. No one seemed to care what happened. Someone had a spasm and cracked a joke—to wit: "Owing to the severity of the summer in and around Jericho, all *white* troops are to be withdrawn, and only the Indians and *Australians* left there." But the Anzacs were too tired to laugh.

Up on the hills of Judaea things were not too bad; life was quite bearable. Soldiers from the line came up to Jerusalem and Bethlehem for a day's spell. Occasionally a few nurses from the Advanced Hospital motored across to see the historic and sacred places. Thus it chanced that one day Robert Blaine—now a lieutenant with a Military Cross Ribbon on his breast—jogged in on his favourite camel to Bethlehem. Perhaps it was destiny, but that very day was the one chosen by Sister Livingstone to go with a party of nurses to see the Church of the Nativity.

Now it would have been quite easy for Flora to have gone in the morning and Bob in the afternoon, or *vice versa;* and they would have escaped or at any rate postponed what happened. But Cupid had been busily watching the pair since the first big Camelier had been carried wounded into Sister's ward at the 14th Australian General Hospital. And Cupid took a hand in shaping their destiny.

Bob had just handed the camel over to his orderly when he noticed the motor-car swing round the corner. And as there were nurses in the car he very naturally waited, and watched them alight. Then he caught sight of Flora, and in a few giant strides was across the road, squeezing her little hands, and rather disconcerting her by the warmth of his welcome. "Sister," he cried; "it's three whole years since I've seen you."

"Three months," she corrected demurely.

"I suppose," he replied, "that you'd say it's too obvious if I said it seemed like three centuries."

"No; I'd say you have been learning pretty speeches from the bints of Palestine."

Having disclaimed such a source of inspiration, Bob was introduced to the two nurses who accompanied Sister, and the old medical officer who accompanied them. But somehow, as they wandered through the ancient Church of the Nativity, the pair became separated from the others. And as the passages down into the crypt were narrow and ill-lighted, he instinctively took her hand in his, and so, hand in hand, humbly and solemnly like two children, they stood before the shrine where, for nearly twenty centuries, pilgrims from all over the world have bent the knee in homage to the Babe of Bethlehem.

Here, according to tradition, stood the stables hewn out of the rock, and used by travellers who stayed at the ancient Khan which, according to trustworthy evidence, did stand hereabouts in the second century. In a recess on the floor is a silver star with the inscription: "*Hic de Virgine Maria Jesus Christus Natus est*" (Here Christ was born of the Virgin Mary).

This is believed to mark the spot of the Nativity. In a manger opposite is the traditional spot where Mary and the Babe received the offerings of the adoration of the Magi. This sacred grotto contains many ancient paintings, and quaint old lamps perpetually burning.

Near by is the tomb of St. Jerome, and in a niche of the wall are little oil lamps always burning. Here an incident occurred which shocked many folk and certainly showed one Australian's absolute lack of reverence and propriety. A guide had been descanting on the various historic sites, and telling wonderful and impossible stories about each. When he came to the tomb of St. Jerome he exclaimed, pointing to a little lamp, "This light has been burning for five hundred years." And one of the listening Anzacs cried, "Well, it's high time it had a spell," and promptly blew out the light. Was it sacrilege, I wonder, or a contempt for and protest against hypocrisy and sham and commercialism that have been superimposed on the simple teachings of the lowly Nazarene?

The nurse and the soldier wandered over the famous Convent of the Nativity, which rears its castle walls high above the surrounding houses. It was built in the year 327 by the Empress Helena or the Emperor Constantine, and has suffered varying fortunes, still remaining one of the chief holy places of the world.

It is probably the oldest Christian church in the world. There are portions of the church assigned to and used for services by the Greek and Armenian Churches, while in the adjoining Church of St. Katharine, the Roman Catholic Church holds its services. Today there was a special service in the Greek Church, and the visitors congregated in the back of the church listening to the beautiful organ, and the children's voices singing the anthem. Somehow the anthem in this spot seemed more inspiring than away at the other end of the world.

The others were not in sight as the Sister and the soldier emerged from the church, so they strolled round the ancient town, visiting the shops where were made the crucifixes and rosaries and various objects of mother-of-pearl and olive wood. Having selected a few souvenirs, they wandered on through the town and out to the Field of the Shepherds.

Here, so tradition hath it, the Angels appeared to the Shepherds and told them of the birth of Jesus. There is a grotto in the field, converted into a chapel, which some devout believers have beautified with pictures of Biblical stories. There was once a mosaic on the floor of the chapel, but it has almost disappeared.

"Here it was," said Blaine, as he emerged into the open air, "that the shepherds watched their flocks, and there"—pointing above—"was the doubtless star of Bethlehem that led the wise men of the East to ..."

For some seconds the soldier gazed with unbelieving eyes into the heavens, his sentence dying away on his lips. The sister watched him in astonishment.

"What ails you?"

"Say, honey," he demanded, "I haven't been drinking, have I?"

"No; why?" she replied.

"Well, can you see a star right overhead?"

"People don't ordinarily see stars at midday."

"So I was thinking," he concurred. "But just you look there."

Flora looked as he pointed above, and then gave a queer little cry of surprise. "Oh, I can see it plainly as anything!"

"That means I'm sober anyhow," said Bob, with a grin. Then for a while they stood silent, gazing at the phenomenon.

"Well, I'm ..." began Bob, and finished lamely, "nonplussed. I've never seen a star before at this hour of the day. Have you?"

"Never," declared Flora.

"Oh well, that's something to talk of when we go back home; but I doubt if people will believe us. I wonder if, by any other chance, that is *the* Star of Bethlehem."

Anon they visited the tomb of Rachel, where very probably Rachel was not buried at all, and the famous Cave of Adullam, where—possibly—David hid from the wrath of his enemies. Here it was that when David expressed a wish for a drink of water from the well where he had so often slaked his thirst when a shepherd lad, that three mighty men of valour from his bodyguard broke through the Philistine ranks and brought him the water. King David was evidently a soldier who inspired his followers with chivalrous devotion.

Here they met again the rest of the party, and proceeded by car to Solomon's Pools for luncheon. These three wonderful reservoirs are a few miles out of Bethlehem, and tradition hath it that they were built by King Solomon to supply Jerusalem with water. Archaeologists, however, ascribe the building to Pontius Pilate. However, the party enjoyed a quiet lunch there, and during the heat of the day rested in the shade of the trees on the terraces They were gathered together, the men smoking, the girls lazily turning the pages of a guidebook, when Blaine turned to Flora and said, "There's the most beautiful sight in the world to be seen from that hill yonder. Will you come?" And Flora rose and followed him.

Hand in hand they climbed the steep ascent, he pausing now and then that she might not be fatigued over-much. Reaching the summit they saw, below, the white houses of Bethlehem, the placid pools of Solomon, the terraced gardens and vineyards of the Judæan hills, and, afar off, the spires and domes and minarets of old Jerusalem.

"Oh, but this is fine," exclaimed Sister.

"Yes," he admitted, "but that is not what I came to see. I came here hoping to see the love-light in a woman's eyes, for that's the most beautiful sight in all the wide world. I'm just an ordinary Australian soldier—but I love you. I have not done anything startling or heroic in this old war—but I love you. I'll never set the Thames afire—but I love you. I've kissed girls before—you're not the first, but you are the last, and I've never before said to any girl, 'I love you.' All that is left of life I place at your disposal, for I love you. To you I shall be more loyal than to any king ; more faithful than to any god, for I love you. Tell me, Flora; do I go back to the front tomorrow just a devil-may-care Anzac, or shall I be the happiest soldier in the whole Empire?"

He took her unresisting hands in his. For a brief second she lifted her love-lit eyes to his. He caught a glimpse of the most beautiful sight in the world. Then he caught her in his arms. . . .

Away down under the trees the genial old Medical Officer, who had been idly scanning the hills through his binoculars, suddenly exclaimed, "Goodness gracious me!"—and promptly put his binoculars back into the case again.

L'Envoi

The Anzac's Farewell to his 'Steed'
In the days when I was younger, when I never knew your worth;
When I thought a prancing palfrey was the finest thing on earth;
When a ride upon a camel seemed a punishment for sin,
And made a man feel fed up with the land we're living in:
It was then my errant fancy lightly turned to thoughts of verse,
And I libelled you, old Hoosta, in a wild iambic curse.
I know you now for better; but for you I might be dead.
So I recant, old Hoosta; I take back all I said.

You have borne me late and early o'er the sands of Sinai,
When the khamseen lashed our faces and our water-bags were dry;
And in the long night marches, when I dozed and dropped the rein,
You somehow found the pathway, and you lobbed in camp again.
All through the mud and slush and mire of rain-soaked Palestine
You struggled like a hero. Now all gratitude is mine.
I once hurled maledictions at your supercilious head—
I'm sorry now, old Hoosta; I take back all I said.

When winter nights were freezing on the hills of old Judaea,
You humped my load of blankets and a ton of surplus gear;
When summer's sun was scorching and my head seemed
  like to burst,
You bore a full fantassie, and quenched my raging thirst.

I have never yet gone hungry, I have never yet gone dry;
That's something to your credit in a place like Sinai.
You have been my board and lodging, you even humped
    my bed—
Honest Injun! Oont, I'm grateful; I take back all I've said.

Once more I'll feel the thrill that only horses give to man,
As I canter gaily onward from Beersheba unto Dan;
I'll sense the dawn-wind's message and the mystery of the stars,
And hear again the music of the bit and snaffle-bars.
So it's farewell now, old Hoosta, our paths diverge from here;
I have got to be a Horseman now, and not a Camelier.
You were smellful, you were ugly. Now I've got a horse instead.
Still, you had the camel virtues, so I take back all I've said.

ALSO FROM LEONAUR
AVAILABLE IN SOFTCOVER OR HARDCOVER WITH DUST JACKET

DOING OUR 'BIT' by *Ian Hay*—Two Classic Accounts of the Men of Kitchener's 'New Army' During the Great War including *The First 100,000* & *All In It*.

AN EYE IN THE STORM by *Arthur Ruhl*—An American War Correspondent's Experiences of the First World War from the Western Front to Gallipoli and Beyond.

STAND & FALL by *Joe Cassells*—A Soldier's Recollections of the 'Contemptible Little Army' and the Retreat from Mons to the Marne, 1914.

RIFLEMAN MACGILL'S WAR by *Patrick MacGill*—A Soldier of the London Irish During the Great War in Europe including *The Amateur Army*, *The Red Horizon* & *The Great Push*.

WITH THE GUNS by *C. A. Rose & Hugh Dalton*—Two First Hand Accounts of British Gunners at War in Europe During World War 1- Three Years in France with the Guns and With the British Guns in Italy.

EAGLES OVER THE TRENCHES by *James R. McConnell & William B. Perry*—Two First Hand Accounts of the American Escadrille at War in the Air During World War 1-Flying For France: With the American Escadrille at Verdun and Our Pilots in the Air.

THE BUSH WAR DOCTOR by *Robert V. Dolbey*—The Experiences of a British Army Doctor During the East African Campaign of the First World War.

THE 9TH—THE KING'S (LIVERPOOL REGIMENT) IN THE GREAT WAR 1914 - 1918 by *Enos H. G. Roberts*—Like many large cities, Liverpool raised a number of battalions in the Great War. Notable among them were the Pals, the Liverpool Irish and Scottish, but this book concerns the wartime history of the 9th Battalion – The Kings.

THE GAMBARDIER by *Mark Severn*—The experiences of a battery of Heavy artillery on the Western Front during the First World War.

FROM MESSINES TO THIRD YPRES by *Thomas Floyd*—A personal account of the First World War on the Western front by a 2/5th Lancashire Fusilier.

THE IRISH GUARDS IN THE GREAT WAR - VOLUME 1 by *Rudyard Kipling*—Edited and Compiled from Their Diaries and Papers Volume 1 The First Battalion.

THE IRISH GUARDS IN THE GREAT WAR - VOLUME 2 by *Rudyard Kipling*—Edited and Compiled from Their Diaries and Papers Volume 2 The Second Battalion.

AVAILABLE ONLINE AT
www.leonaur.com
AND OTHER GOOD BOOK STORES

ALSO FROM LEONAUR
AVAILABLE IN SOFTCOVER OR HARDCOVER WITH DUST JACKET

ARMOURED CARS IN EDEN by *K. Roosevelt*—An American President's son serving in Rolls Royce armoured cars with the British in Mesopatamia & with the American Artillery in France during the First World War.

CHASSEUR OF 1914 by *Marcel Dupont*—Experiences of the twilight of the French Light Cavalry by a young officer during the early battles of the great war in Europe.

TROOP HORSE & TRENCH by *R.A. Lloyd*—The experiences of a British Lifeguardsman of the household cavalry fighting on the western front during the First World War 1914-18.

THE LONG PATROL by *George Berrie*—A Novel of Light Horsemen from Gallipoli to the Palestine campaign of the First World War.

THE EAST AFRICAN MOUNTED RIFLES by *C.J. Wilson*—Experiences of the campaign in the East African bush during the First World War

THE FIGHTING CAMELIERS by *Frank Reid*—The exploits of the Imperial Camel Corps in the desert and Palestine campaigns of the First World War.

WITH THE IMPERIAL CAMEL CORPS IN THE GREAT WAR by *Geoffrey Inchbald*—The story of a serving officer with the British 2nd battalion against the Senussi and during the Palestine campaign.

STEEL CHARIOTS IN THE DESERT by *S.C. Rolls*—The first world war experiences of a Rolls Royce armoured car driver with the Duke of Westminster in Libya and in Arabia with T.E. Lawrence.

INFANTRY BRIGADE: 1914 by *Edward Gleichen*—The Diary of a Commander of the 15th Infantry Brigade, 5th Division, British Army, During the Retreat from Mons

HEARTS & DRAGONS by *Charles R. M. F. Crutwell*—The 4th Royal Berkshire Regiment in France and Italy During the Great War, 1914-1918.

TIGERS ALONG THE TIGRIS by *E. J. Thompson*—The Leicestershire Regiment in Mesopotamia During the First World War.

DESPATCH RIDER by *W. H. L. Watson*—The Experiences of a British Army Motorcycle Despatch Rider During the Opening Battles of the Great War in Europe.

AVAILABLE ONLINE AT
www.leonaur.com
AND OTHER GOOD BOOK STORES

ALSO FROM LEONAUR
AVAILABLE IN SOFTCOVER OR HARDCOVER WITH DUST JACKET

A JOURNAL OF THE SECOND SIKH WAR by *Daniel A. Sandford*—The Experiences of an Ensign of the 2nd Bengal European Regiment During the Campaign in the Punjab, India, 1848-49.

LAKE'S CAMPAIGNS IN INDIA by *Hugh Pearse*—The Second Anglo Maratha War, 1803-1807. Often neglected by historians and students alike, Lake's Indian campaign was fought against a resourceful and ruthless enemy-almost always superior in numbers to his own forces.

BRITAIN IN AFGHANISTAN 1: THE FIRST AFGHAN WAR 1839-42 by *Archibald Forbes*—Following over a century of the gradual assumption of sovereignty of the Indian Sub-Continent, the British Empire, in the form of the Honourable East India Company, supported by troops of the new Queen Victoria's army, found itself inevitably at the natural boundaries that surround Afghanistan. There it set in motion a series of disastrous events-the first of which was to march into the country at all.

BRITAIN IN AFGHANISTAN 2: THE SECOND AFGHAN WAR 1878-80 by *Archibald Forbes*—This the history of the Second Afghan War-another episode of British military history typified by savagery, massacre, siege and battles.

UP AMONG THE PANDIES by *Vivian Dering Majendie*—An outstanding account of the campaign for the fall of Lucknow. This is a vital book of war as fought by the British Army of the mid-nineteenth century, but in truth it is also an essential book of war that will enthral.

BLOW THE BUGLE, DRAW THE SWORD by *W. H. G. Kingston*—The Wars, Campaigns, Regiments and Soldiers of the British & Indian Armies During the Victorian Era, 1839-1898.

INDIAN MUTINY 150th ANNIVERSARY: A LEONAUR ORIGINAL

MUTINY: 1857 by *James Humphries*—It is now 150 years since the 'Indian Mutiny' burst like an engulfing flame on the British soldiers, their families and the civilians of the Empire in North East India. The Bengal Native army arose in violent rebellion, and the once peaceful countryside became a battleground as Native sepoys and elements of the Indian population massacred their British masters and defeated them in open battle. As the tide turned, a vengeful army of British and loyal Indian troops repressed the insurgency with a savagery that knew no mercy. It was a time of fear and slaughter. James Humphries has drawn together the voices of those dreadful days for this commemorative book.

AVAILABLE ONLINE AT
www.leonaur.com
AND OTHER GOOD BOOK STORES

www.ingramcontent.com/pod-product-compliance
Lightning Source LLC
Chambersburg PA
CBHW030502110426
42738CB00054B/487